Towns for people

Towns for people

Transforming urban life

Ken Worpole

for Comedia and
The Gulbenkian Foundation (UK)

Open University Press
Buckingham · Philadelphia

Open University Press
Celtic Court
22 Ballmoor
Buckingham
MK18 1XW

and
1900 Frost Road, Suite 101
Bristol, PA 19007, USA

First Published 1992

A catalogue record of this book is available
from the British Library.

Library of Congress Cataloging-in-Publication Data

Worpole, Ken.
        Towns for people : transforming urban life / Ken Worpole.
            p.   cm.
        Includes bibliographical references and index.
        ISBN 0–335–09965–3. — ISBN 0–335–09964–5 (pb)
        1. Central business districts.   2. Central business districts —
Great Britain.   3. City and town life.   4. City and town life —
Great Britain.   5. Public spaces.   6. Public spaces—Great
Britain.   7. Leisure.   8. Leisure—Great Britain.   I. Title.
HT170.W675   1992
307.76—dc20
                                                            91–44947
                                                                CIP

Typeset by Inforum Typesetting, Portsmouth
Printed in Great Britain by St Edmundsbury Press
Bury St Edmunds, Suffolk

Contents

Introduction

'I have also thought of a model city from which I deduce all others,' Marco Polo answered. 'It is a city made only of exceptions, exclusions, incongruities, contradictions. If such a city is the most improbable, by reducing the number of elements, we increase the probability that the city really exists . . . But I cannot force my operation beyond a certain limit: I would achieve cities too probable to be real.'

Italo Calvino, Invisible Cities *(1979)*

This book is about the crisis facing British towns and cities. It follows a 15-month study of twelve towns – Basingstoke, Feltham (London Borough of Hounslow), Gloucester, Luton, Manchester, Middlesbrough, Preston, Reading, Southend, Stirling, Swansea, Woolwich (London Borough of Greenwich) – by Comedia Consultancy for the Gulbenkian Foundation (UK). The study was commissioned in response to rising concern at the way in which town centres were perceived locally and nationally as having lost many of their traditional functions – as meeting places, as centres of social, political and cultural life and as the very focus of the urban 'public realm' – becoming simply shopping and commercial centres by day and near-deserted ghost towns by night. A pilot study to test the methodology had earlier been carried out in Liverpool city centre.

Early work by Comedia and its associates, particularly studies carried out on leisure policy for South East Economic Development Strategy (SEEDS) in Basildon, Brighton, Crawley, Harlow,

1

Oxford and Stevenage, published as *On the Town* (Worpole 1987), alerted us to the issue of 'dead town centres at night'. Further qualitative studies about why people did or did not attend arts venues in Islington, and a number of other pieces of market research, revealed that the leisure choices made by people could no longer be separated from their fear of going out at night, from the availability of reliable public transport, or from the effective kind of marketing which addresses those new kinds of cultural identity acquired in a more consumerist and cosmopolitan society.

This prompted the pamphlet *City Centres, City Cultures* (Bianchini *et al.* 1988) as a first attempt to outline the issues and advocate an arts-based approach to revitalization. Further work on local authority tourism strategies in South-East England, published as *The Last Resort* (Landry *et al.* 1989), continued to focus on the town centre as a key site for civic and cultural renewal. It was at this point that Charles Landry of Comedia and I met with Iain Reid of the Gulbenkian Foundation to discuss the possibility of a specific research project designed to test many of the assumptions being made about town-centre decline, a proposal that Iain Reid and the then Gulbenkian Director, L.C. Taylor, decided to back with enthusiasm – and a grant!

The project clearly struck a national chord. Letters inviting local authorities to participate brought a quick and ready response, and from a short-list of some 50 towns initially contacted, a dozen representing a geographical spread across Britain and a range of population sizes with varying demographic features were finally chosen. The towns contributed towards the cost of the study, adding to the core grant from the Gulbenkian Foundation. The brief was to examine the economic, social and cultural life of each town centre, with particular attention being paid to its use at night and at weekends.

At the end of the research, each town was presented with its own confidential report. Many of the reports were quite critical of local authority policy, but they also contained detailed recommendations for action and renewal. Most local authorities not only accepted the criticisms made, but quite quickly took action on some of the suggestions contained in the individual reports, and in the case studies of best practice contained in the Summary Report, *Out of Hours* (Comedia 1991). The report outlined the main issues emerging from the study and contained over 100 examples of 'best practice' in urban renewal. The report gained national attention and was reported at length in the national press, including wide coverage and discussion on radio and television and in many specialist journals. The issue was clearly one which had become a matter of widespread public concern.

I believe that the *Out of Hours* study marked a qualitative leap forward in contemporary urban policy and analysis, for it was rooted in the daily experiences of the more than one thousand people who talked to us in the 12 towns, and in the comments and experiences of more than 400 voluntary organizations. In each town we interviewed not only councillors and local government officers but also police officers, local businessmen, nightclub owners, publicans, church leaders, ethnic minority leaders, local historians and archivists, representatives of women's organizations and of youth organizations, and hundreds of individuals encountered on the street, in pubs and clubs, or by arrangement in their homes. Researchers spent time touring towns and cities in the early morning in police patrol cars, or visited pubs, restaurants and clubs along with everybody else and walked the streets until the last town-centre reveller had gone home.

So this study was less about architecture, planning, policing, problems of social control, or the politics of urban economic development or renewal, and more about the lived experience of urban life in Britain in the 1990s. It was about the tenuous but also tenacious links and loyalties which still exist between people and places, and also about the obvious urban tensions surrounding the decline of the public realm. For on any level or scale of measurement, by the end of the study it did seem clear that the public domain in British towns and cities – as public space, as public access in and around town centres, as freedom of movement or association for all citizens (particularly, though, for women at night), as diversity and choice in leisure and as participation in local civic debate – seemed in decline, and certainly more restricted than in many other European towns and cities.

For while we did not subscribe to the notion of a golden age of provincial culture and popular democracy, all the evidence showed that Victorian towns and cities had a much more developed range of public buildings, public markets, festivals and popular civic traditions and organizations than their late twentieth-century counterparts. A main concern of this book is to examine all of the pressures, changes in lifestyle, economic, social and cultural factors which produced this decline of the urban public sphere, a decline partly masked by the confusion which exists in Britain over the definitions attached to the distinct associations of 'towns' and 'cities', a distinction with no material basis left at all. For the purpose of the study and of this book, 'town' and 'city' are interchangeable terms. In Britain city status is awarded by the Crown and bears little or no relation to size, geographical or contemporary regional importance. In medieval Germany corporate status was awarded to any town with more than 600 inhabitants; the city-states of medieval Tuscany often had no more than 20,000 inhabitants. None of the towns or cities we studied had a population of less than 120,000.

The emphasis of the study, and this book, is specifically on the town centre. We chose to concentrate on town centres for several reasons. First, town centres were often the focus of civic identity, expressing the essence of what each town was and how it was different from others. Street markets, town squares, business districts, meeting places, festivals and fairs, carnivals and other local celebrations often distinguished the associations people had with the town centre compared with associations with outlying districts.

Second, town centres still retain many of the most important architectural assets: from Stirling Castle to Middlesbrough Town Hall or Preston's elegant Harris Library and Museum; from Liverpool's St George's Hall and two great cathedrals to Southend's elegant Clifftown; from Swansea's curving Wind Street to Woolwich's rococo town hall or solid Arsenal, town centres usually contained the most important public buildings. Town halls, libraries, museums and art galleries, cathedrals and churches, Mechanics' Institutes, almshouses and banqueting halls, schools and chapels, bath-houses and covered markets: the very best architecture of many towns is located in the town centre. It seemed important to ask why these architectural assets should be conserved or preserved in a social vacuum?

Third, the town centre remains for many people important neutral public territory, a site where people can mix and mingle without feeling socially embarrassed, where to some degree everybody is equal for a while, and only dress appears the main difference. As we found, there are now few if any 'one-class' towns in Britain; each may have had a predominance of one social class, but this was always moderated by a significant ethnic or student population, or by different cultural styles connected with age rather than social background. The majority of people still feel that the town centre belongs to everybody, whereas much other commercial or residential space is regarded as off-territory, or belonging to someone else.

Fourth, the town centre represents cosmopolitan values: many British towns and cities contain significant ethnic populations. It is invariably in the town centre that cosmopolitan values seem most evident, particularly in social and leisure activities – restaurants, night-clubs, street markets – even though, as noted, there are still real difficulties in some places for Black and Asian residents to participate fully in civic and economic life. It was also noted that many new immigrant populations had settled in town-centre or inner-city areas – the Chinese and Afro-Caribbean communities in Liverpool, Middlesbrough's Asian population, Manchester's Chinatown – and these were often among the liveliest places at night in towns.

Fifth, that town centres remain key transport hubs; in all the towns we studied, the main BR stations and bus stations were located in or adjacent to the town centre, and were often significant meeting places for people, often despite their poor facilities.

Sixth, certain public facilities and services need to achieve a critical mass of numbers if they are to function effectively. Theatres, cinemas, swimming pools, reference libraries, information centres, art galleries and meeting rooms are still usually located in town centres where they should be supported and their roles enhanced. Suburban districts cannot justify such a range of services.

Seventh, town centres are a focus for 'the evening economy' which it was felt was severely underdeveloped in Britain compared

5

with other European countries. It seemed astonishing that the difference in levels of usage of town centres between daytime and night-time was so great. In Liverpool for example, it was found that the same street corner might register 15,000 people passing each hour during the day, but only 200 passers-by each hour at night. As evidence mounts as to the potential importance of the arts and leisure economy, it was strongly felt that the evening economy in many towns was ideally located in the town centre where most of the pubs, restaurants and leisure facilities were, even though underused or currently closed during the evening.

Eighth, the town centre is a key site for visitors and tourists: many towns and cities have begun to develop tourism policies in order to take advantage of the economic benefits associated with leisure spending. Although the attractions may not be based in the town centres, for visitors arriving by public transport the town centre is the first point of contact. It is also where the shops are if it rains and the picnic, excursion or day on the beach has to be cancelled. Thriving town centres are essential to tourism strategies. In several interviews, hotel managers indicated that many visitors do not leave their hotels in the evening because they believe there is nothing to do in town.

During the period of the research the 'problem' of the town centre was being discussed elsewhere with increasing concern: in connection with the threat posed by out-of-town retailing, in connection with the Home Office Safer Cities project, in the growing concern with youth drinking and town-centre violence, in the growing concern that public facilities – transport, libraries, sports centres, adult education – were deteriorating as a result of local government cuts, and certainly with regard to the effects of the recession on town-centre retailing. All of these factors are included in this study, but in the end the book returns again and again to what turned out to be our principle conceptual framework and concern – that the relationship between people and places, between citizenship and public space, the values of cultural diversity and cosmopolitanism, the very essence of what living in towns and cities was all about, had been lost in a preoccupation with land-use planning and 'race-to-the-finish' local economic and social growth. Too little monitoring or reflection was built into the planning or development process; too little consultation had been undertaken; too little concern had been given to incremental political processes as opposed to once-and-for-all decision-making, whose effects would be left to another generation to sort out.

This book is a more considered elaboration of the issues raised by the *Out of Hours* report. It owes much to the work of the many people associated with Comedia who worked on it, notably Jenny Beerbohm, Clive Bell, Fred Brookes, Liz Cooper, Adele Dawson, Evelyn Hamilton, Jonathan Hyams, Anne James, Owen Kelly, Liz Masebo, John Montgomery, John Punter and Phyllida Shaw. Franco Bianchini, Liz Greenhalgh and Charles Landry deserve special mention: Franco for undertaking the pilot study in Liverpool which provided the project with many of its intellectual bearings; and Liz and Charles for consistently raising new issues and questions throughout the research when it would have been easier to smooth out the complexities with rhetoric and fine writing.

We are most grateful for the support throughout the study of officers in the towns involved, particularly George Crowe (Southend), Julian Farrall (Basingstoke), Geoff Filkin and Peter Fieldhouse (Reading), David Grace and Trevor Osborne (Swansea), Arthur McCourt and Iain Whitelaw (Stirling), Brian Manning and Hugh McLorry (Preston), Tom Russell (Manchester), Erica Lander (Central Manchester Development Corporation), David Taylor (Greenwich), David Wright and Tony Noble (Middlesbrough), Phillip Cooke (Gloucester), Geoff Allen (Hounslow) and Mike Drew (Luton). Thanks are also due to the invaluable advice offered by the Advisory Board: Robert Davies (Business in the Community), Paul Davies (The Civic Trust), Jean Carr (SRU Ltd), Lesley Ginsburg, Roger Graef, Professor Patsy Healey, Judy Hillman, Dr David Jenkins, Bishop of Durham, David Nicholson Lord, Professor Bikhu Parekh, Michael Parkinson (University of Liverpool) and, last but not least, Ben Whitaker, Director of the Gulbenkian Foundation.

This book, therefore, is the result of many people's work, and in taking the credit for writing it I am also more than happy to accept the blame for any factual errors, misjudgements, and intellectual confusions which may be found in it, as I am sure there will be. This was new territory for many of us, particularly myself, and if at times the study takes on more the flavour of travellers' tales rather than sociological analysis, at least it reports that although there was much wrong with British towns and cities, there was also much going on that indicated a willingness to learn from past mistakes and get it right this time. And if at times the book appears to place too much emphasis on the role of local authorities, it is because I personally believe that democratically elected local government, flawed though it may be, remains the best system for administering towns and cities yet found. The majority of people in Britain, as in the rest of the world, now live in towns and cities and will continue to do so in future. Urban policy is no longer a dry-as-dust matter for academics and planners: it concerns the future of us all.

1

What went wrong?

Too many eggshells and too few omelettes.
> J.B. Priestley, English Journey *1934*

The French National Assembly contains the most experienced collection of urban planners in the world. Nearly every MP is either a mayor of a city, town or village, or a regional departmental councillor. But there were barely 100 MPs on the benches when the Prime Minister, Michel Rocard, un-folded a plan which was followed by the appointment of a Minister of Towns. This caution was inspired by a general recognition that urban policy has been the greatest single failure in the past decade.
> Paul Webster, The Guardian *(31st December 1990)*

The future of towns and cities is one of the most important issues on the British and European political agenda today. Eighty per cent of Europe now lives in towns and cities, but what urban living is precisely about – what it is and what it could be – remains an unanswered question. In Britain, it has been argued, both Right and Left political ideologies have incorporated a dislike of cities; the Right because they believe that urban life is too closely associated with rioting, ungrateful populations and unsavoury ideas; the Left because a dominant strand of British socialist theory has been rural and arcadian in tone and aspiration rather than urban. Both would build their utopian societies, if they could, on green field sites, in rustic hamlets and sturdy villages.

Modern urban life is often regarded as an ersatz form of experience that has to be buttressed by programmes of urban aid, short-term government schemes for economic and social amelioration, grants for gentrification, and additional policing, even as local government strategic powers continue to be eroded. Participation in local politics is seen as 'parish pump politics', a form of activity or voluntary commitment only slightly more serious than scouting or train-spotting. Few local politicians have caught the public attention since Joe Chamberlain with his 'civic gospel' in Birmingham in the nineteenth century, with the possible exception of Herbert Morrison at the London County Council, David Blunkett in Sheffield in the 1970s, Ken Livingstone at the Greater London Council (GLC) and Lady Porter at Westminster Council, the latter two as figures of mockery and press derision. Worse still are the negative images now associated with the phrase 'inner city', once one of the most prestigious places in which to live but now stereotyped as a human and social mire. To add to the stigma associated with urban life, we now have monitoring.

Of the ranking of towns and cities there suddenly appears to be no end. In recent years there have been the Glasgow University surveys, which in 1988 produced a league table of the 'quality of life' in the 38 largest British cities and in 1989 a second table ranking 34 of Britain's 'intermediate cities'; in 1990 Reading University published its list of Europe's 117 most prosperous cities, and in the same month researchers from the University of Newcastle upon Tyne and the University of Wales produced a list ranking the economic prosperity of 280 towns and cities in Britain. All of these studies are of interest, particularly to the towns involved, but all of them are marked by the one great drawback of statistical empiricism: that the human element is noticeably missing. For these are rankings of the externalities, important as they certainly are, but none of the studies involved asking the people who lived in these towns and cities how they actually felt about how and where they lived. It is precisely the lived experience of the urban milieux which is the main concern of this book: how urbanism can be something more than the sum of the statistical parts and become a qualitative understanding of social, cultural and political well-being.

The work now being put into these systems of ranking indicates that a growing spirit of urban competitiveness is at work. What underpins these league tables is the need to attract and retain mobile multinational investment capital, trained labour, government grants, tourists, office relocations, new housing and commercial developments, in an increasingly competitive world. These are crucial elements in the rise and fall of modern towns and cities, but they do not of themselves address the question of the qualitative importance of urban experience. This question will not go away, and it cannot be defined from the outside. What does living in a successful town or city involve for the people who live there, and what qualities of life and opportunities are available to them that are not available elsewhere? In short, why do so many people still choose to live in towns?

Starting points: arrivals and departures

For the researchers, not unsurprisingly, the starting point for each case study was the experience of arriving in a town (in some cases known beforehand, in others completely new), and this often happened to exhibit one of the worst examples of neglect. The obvious fact is that town and city centres are the main point of arrival and departure for residents and visitors alike, whether at the British Rail station, bus station, or multi-storey car park, yet it was noted how poor and unattractive these facilities often were, some of them so uninviting that many visitors could be forgiven for getting back in the train, bus or car and heading home again.

Few BR stations displayed maps of the town centre or any kind of directions to local places or facilities. Few gave any indication at all of what was on offer in or attractive about the town one had arrived in. Preston station posed immense problems for disabled users – an (at times) unstaffed station with 62 steps to be tackled to get to and from the platform where the Blackpool trains stop. Woolwich station from the outside (admittedly prior to refurbishment) was boarded up for months and gave no indication that it was even a station. In Southend the two main stations provided no welcome to visitors, directions into the town or any kind of interaction with the town centre; Southend Central station had a forecourt that was used for staff parking rather than for priority taxi or pedestrian access. Swansea station, though having a babyroom with nappy-changing facilities, and a small but pleasant booking hall, opened out immediately into a taxi-rank/car park where the pedestrian risked life and limb to get onto a safe pavement and walk into town.

Bus stations were often worse: exposed to the elements, with cattle-market metal waiting bays where buses waited blowing diesel fumes into the faces of the patient queues, poor-quality information, timetables that required a degree in statistical probability to decode, few if any seats, little or no information about the surrounding district, few if any street maps. Bus transport, the preserve of the elderly, schoolchildren and women with children, has been so downgraded that it is used only under the most desperate conditions. Yet people stayed loyal to them as meeting places in some towns. In Southend, we were told, the au pairs meet up at the bus station. In Middlesbrough the new bus station is a popular meeting place, with a café and information centre, telephones and toilets. Even so, students going there late at night to catch a bus or coach were often escorted there by other students who waited until they were safely on board. Preston bus station has a Baby Day Room. The British architect, Ralph Erskine, has shown the potential of such places with his marvellous Central Bus Depot in Stockholm, where passengers are kept quite separate from the buses until the moment of departure, electronic notice-boards give up-to-date information about arrivals and departures, and there are things to do while waiting.

Multistorey car parks now have their own place in the demonology of British urban folklore. In most cases poorly-lit by day or night, people regarded them with fear and loathing. Dirt and graffiti gave them a violent ambience, and much town centre crime was directly attributable to breaking into and stealing from cars in multistorey car parks. Some were more pleasant than others: the best we found was in Middlesbrough where a three-year-old multistorey had been kept as new, free of dirt and litter, and relatively light inside. Multistorey car parks are not conducive to short-stay parking. Even in very small centres, the multistorey ethos dominates. In Feltham the small town-centre car park, which should be easy, convenient and quick, small enough to supervise and deter vandalism, has all the negative features of a large-city multistorey. Short of knocking them all down and starting again, we recommended that in each town one multistorey car park was chosen as a model and refurbished to a higher standard, with better lighting, more staff, and women-only bays at ground-floor level which if successful, would encourage further investment in the others. The model car park in each town would be the one staffed and open in the evening.

The experience of deciphering towns anew, as outsiders, highlighted three of the main pressures which have historically affected urban life most profoundly in the past two decades:

- the domination of transport by the private car;
- the impact of the 'retail revolution';
- and the privatization of leisure.

These appear to be among the most important explanations of what went wrong, and are therefore the focus for this opening chapter.

Traffic in towns

If the town centre is now back as the key site of the urban policy advocated here, what happened to nearly destroy this cornerstone of urban life, or, in the words of J.B. Priestley, why did so many broken eggs and so few omelettes emerge from urban redevelopment in post-war Britain?

Much blame has been wrongly attributed to the influential report *Traffic in Towns*, produced by Colin Buchanan for the Ministry of Transport (1963). Buchanan's report anticipated the dangers to traditional town environments by the growth of car ownership, but unfortunately only some of his recommendations were ever acted upon. Not only did the report recommend new urban roads, ring roads and bypasses, it also came out strongly in favour of local government control of car parking numbers, charges and locations, as well as an expanded system of 'good, cheap public transport', and a staggering of working hours to avoid the early morning and early evening traffic jams which made urban life so unpleasant. Many of the ring roads were built, effectively cutting off many town centres from their residential hinterlands, but the recommendations for the control of car usage by heavy parking charges, improved and cheaper public transport and a number of other measures came to nothing. The motor-industry lobby, ever powerful, lobbied for roads, cheap car parking and an end to subsidized public transport. Bus passenger traffic declined nationally from 42 per cent of all journeys in 1953 to just 8 per cent in 1983. The effects are evident in every town and city in Britain today.

The impact of the car on modern towns has for the most part been disastrous. Ring roads have created major psychological barriers to walking or cycling in and out of town centres even from residential areas only 10 minutes' walking distance from the centre. In Preston we talked to people living on housing estates only a few minutes' walk away from the town centre who would never consider walking because of the physical and psychological obstacle courses involved. Pedestrian underpasses, tunnels, steps, broken pavements, traffic lights programmed at busy junctions to allow no more than seven seconds for pedestrians to cross (and some which allow pedestrians no time at all), have created major barriers to walking, particularly for those with pushchairs or for the disabled.

The use of cars to travel even short distances to work has meant the giving over of large areas of town-centre land to daytime car parking; at night these open car parks become bleak and wind-swept wastelands. In Basingstoke, the town-centre sports centre found that customers within easy walking distance preferred to drive. Some residential areas in Basingstoke have no obvious walking route into town. Multistorey car parks, again busy by day but mostly empty at night, have become the new dragons' lairs of urban folklore. In Southend a council officer asked quizzically why it was that so many people who used the swimming pools, gyms and sports centres to keep fit all arrived in cars, even from the neighbouring residential areas. In Middlesbrough a woman told us that people used cars to travel to the next street.

Both the Civic Trust and the Town and Country Planning Association (TCPA) have warned against the continuing despoliation of Britain's town and city centres by car traffic; in August 1990 the Civic Trust published an environmental audit of 50 British cities which found that traffic congestion was the major issue; David Hall of the TCPA has described towns such as St Albans, Watford and Dorking as becoming 'filled with multi-storey car parks'. For the architect, Richard Rogers (Campbell 1989), 'Traffic is the big city problem of the 20th century; it cuts cities up in all directions.' British Rail remains hopelessly confused about its own policy on bikes on trains, an alliance of interests that potentially could be both environmentally effective and profitable.

Walking in towns and cities has been undervalued and often ignored by planners. Most traffic research fails to statistically register walking as a form of transport, even though half the journeys made within towns are made on foot. The people who walk are, not surprisingly, those who probably most need some form of assisted transport – research has shown that young men walk least and old women and young children walk most. The use of the car is inversely related to the need for it! Although shopping is regarded as one of the great pleasures of contemporary culture, according to the National Consumer Council (1987), 'for many hundreds of thousands of consumers it is little short of a nightmare. They are the low income families, the single parent families, the elderly, the disabled and the non-car owners.' A survey in Milton Keynes showed that three-quarters of housewives do not have access to the family car during weekdays. Few 'decision-makers' in the towns we studied had recently walked in and around the town centre, and it was nearly always assumed we had 'had trouble parking' when we visited planners and politicians in their offices, even though we invariably travelled by public transport.

Safety issues are also involved. Britain prides itself on its comparatively low car-accident rate, but this is for car-occupant safety only; compared with the rest of the European Community only Spain, Portugal and Greece have worse pedestrian fatality rates, and the UK has the highest rate for children.

The need to look to Europe for ideas about urban futures is certainly great with regard to solving outstanding issues of traffic in towns. Peter Hall's 1990 TCPA lecture described the case of Germany where:

In every city – in Munich, in Stuttgart, in Frankfurt – they have built magnificent new public transport systems: underground railways and suburban trains that tunnel under the city centres.

In every one, virtually the whole city centre has been turned into a pedestrian precinct, an oasis of peace and calm from which the car has been banished and people walk free. The streets are bursting with life; the crowds are almost overwhelming. They are happy, relaxed, carefree crowds.

Just off-centre, in the older inner residential districts, they have now adopted a different battery of tactics. The traffic is being calmed by making it drive at walking speed; main streets are actually being narrowed to provide more space for pedestrians and bikes.

Elsewhere, bikes have their own lanes at the kerb side of the pavement: a device we adopted along our arterial roads in the 1930s, and then allowed to fall into disuse. The sheer volume of bike traffic is amazing. The cities are being won back for people.

In Germany traffic calming has reduced pedestrian accidents to 5 per cent of their previous level, and in Copenhagen provision for cyclists has recently doubled to 9 per cent the number of journeys to work made by bicycle. Patterns in urban mobility are changing fast. This is why we can no longer take the car-strangled city or town centre as a given; within a decade many towns, like Brighton and Oxford already, will have banned non-essential car traffic in the town centres. Where will the new urban dynamic come from? What will we do with the spaces left behind?

The retail revolution

The second major impact on town-centre usage in the post-war era was the phenomenal effect of the 'retail revolution' which swept through Britain in the 1970s and 1980s. The revolution involved widespread physical alterations to the built fabric of most towns and cities, and changes in local economic leverage, involving: pedestrianization of high streets; development of covered shopping centres; appropriation and ownership of town centres by pension funds and insurance companies; creation of closed, private spaces in town centres where public thorough-fares and pedestrian routes once used to be; escalation of town-centre rents so that only multiples could afford to be there; requirement for large-scale dedicated car parking space; growth of the financial services sector in high-street premises (building societies, cash-dispensing machines); decline of secondary shop-ping areas; decline of town-centre housing and residential ac-commodation; and finally the marginalization of town-centre districts where traditional facilities (libraries, museums, theatres) were sited, as shopping centres created new centres of critical mass elsewhere. The effects of this transformation of many town and city centres are still being lived through. But changes of attitude were involved too. As Daniel Bell (1979) once argued: 'The greatest single engine in the destruction of the Protestant ethic was the invention of the instalment plan, or instant credit.'

In 1986 the personal assets of the British public went into the red for the first time ever: borrowings exceeded savings by nearly £20 billion and by March 1988 the amount of outstan-ding consumer debt was £38 billion, about £2000 per house-hold. Credit itself is not wrong and most people have handled it sensibly. The reason for most personal debt problems, which is becoming a social problem of some magnitude, is not over-spending but a sudden change in personal circumstances – the loss of a job, a rise in mortgage interest rates, marriage failure or some other event. But the amount of money committed to consumption has left little for activities of a more participatory nature.

Town centres have appeared to move from multifunctional areas (government and commercial administration, artisanal pro-duction, service industries, religious worship, civic buildings and public entertainment, housing) towards monofunctionalism (shopping). In the process of change from urban production and administration to consumption, Bell (1979) has argued, some of the political and ethical functions of urban civic life have been lost. Planning has responded to these changes rather than at-tempting to intervene in the process of city-building. Peter

Buchanan (1988) has argued that 'British planning is predicated upon a desperately impoverished conceptual model of the city. In essence that model (when planning still had some life and credibility) was consumerist rather than civic.' Planning responded to the car, responded to the in-town and out-of-town shopping centre, rather than seeking to shape the urban mix. One of the people interviewed in Preston said: 'The town centre is planned on the basis that no one respectable is out at night.'

The sheer scale of the impact of retailing cannot be underestimated. Between 1965 and 1986 developers built 660 new shopping centres averaging 153,000 square feet, roughly one new centre for every 80,000 people, which means often more than one new centre in every medium-sized town. In 1967 there was only one superstore in Britain; by 1983 there were 289. In 1977 there were less than 40 DIY warehouses in Britain; by 1987 there were over 600. The year 1988 was a record year for retail park openings, with 45 schemes completed, providing 5,765,000 square feet of floorspace.

The locational effects in towns centres of this proliferation of shopping centres have often been disastrous. In Swansea, the High Street has almost been abandoned as new shopping centres have opened to the south of the city, and the main public library and fine Glynn Vivian Art Gallery have been left stranded on the northern town-centre perimeter. In Luton the Arndale centre blocks all pedestrian routes through the town centre, as does the main shopping centre in Basingstoke; in both towns the main pedestrian route to the main BR station involves walking through the private property of the shopping centre. In Basildon the opening of the Eastgate Centre shifted the 'centre' of the town east and left the new Towngate Theatre, main library, town church and municipal buildings relatively isolated.

Apart from the environmental impact of the centres, the local economic impact has been felt, too. The success of the multiples has been at the expense of local retailing, service industries and even production. Only the multiples have been able to afford the rent in the new malls and high street locations and local firms have been driven out of business. Between 1960 and 1989 the multiples increased their share of the retailing sales from 33 per cent to 80 per cent, giving them the giant's share of the market and of the town centre.

It was rare to find in or near town-centre sites, specialist shops such as picture framers, craft and artists' materials, health-food shops, antiques, wine-making and home brewing, cycle shops, hobby shops, radio repairers, second-hand bookshops, and many of the other shops that reflect an active participation in leisure. In Truro most of the local traders who accounted for nearly 80 per cent of shops and stalls, have vanished from the city centre. In Southend people complained that it was no longer possible to buy a pint of milk in the High Street; in Basingstoke people said it was difficult to buy a tin of paint. There were many complaints that in the large retail chains, shop staff were untrained and were often selling products – cameras, hi-fi equipment, tools, sports equipment – that they neither knew about nor understood. The displacement of other activities can be seen most graphically in the case of Bath where, in 1988, crane manutfacturers Stothert & Pitt, one of the West Country's oldest firms, learned that it was to be broken up and and sold by its new owners to release its 15-acre town-centre site for re-development; high land values had made the site much more valuable for shops, offices and leisure facilities than for manufacturing.

Retailing in Bath has been the subject of much discussion, with a 41 per cent increase in retail floorspace in the city between 1975 and 1987. 'Luxury shopping, once merely one of a profusion of treats, has become the city's *raison d'être*,' wrote Frances Anderton (1989), 'Bath is an extreme beneficiary and victim of a market economy and retailing revolution that threaten to overrun the entire nation with useless, aka luxury goods, shops and leave a trail of urban erosion in their wake.' Most of Bath's established stores have gone, and the multiples now occupy 104 sites in the main trading streets, compared with only 24 independents. However, such was the vulnerability of this luxury retailing to trade winds, that the combination of the uniform business rate and a downturn in the economy meant that 80 town-centre shops closed in 1990.

The owners of the shopping malls often have no direct interest in retailing, and certainly not in the life of the towns they are located in, for the majority of owners are pension funds and insurance companies which have invested in retail property as part of a wider portfolio. The main shopping centre in Basingstoke is owned by the Prudential; in Reading it is owned by Legal & General; in Stirling by Standard Life; in Preston the St George's shopping centre is owned by Legal & General and the Fishergate Centre by Charterhouse Securities; in Southend a local land developer, Southend Estates, was bought out by Higgs & Hill. Their interest in the towns their money is invested in is remote if not non-existent; it is a financial relationship only, and only questions of the long-term economic viability of town-centre retailing will bring these companies to the local civic table. As Michael Middleton (1987) noted: 'Although 20% of British pension funds are invested in property, their investment capacity has rarely been used for revitalisation.' In England and Wales at least, there is no longer any local or regional capital source, no Luton Bank or Bank of Swansea. In America and many West European countries, local and regional banks continue to play an important part in urban renewal.

We also noted the effects of multiple ownership of retailing on staff attitudes among shop workers, who now constitute one of the largest groups of workers in the town centre. Much modern retail work is part-time, low-paid, unskilled and often highly casualized. In Swansea, for example, where we looked at retail workers' conditions in detail, part-time jobs accounted for two-thirds of all retail employment, with 85 per cent of the staff of firms like Marks & Spencer part-time. Two-thirds of all retail jobs were held by women. In Preston 26% of all town-centre employment was made up of part-time women's jobs.

For shop workers, coming into the town centre every day was no different from going to work in a factory. We realized that if attitudes towards seeing the town centre as a lively, public site for leisure and recreation were to change, then town-centre workers could play a key role as 'ambassadors' for urban renewal. Making them aware of – and even giving them discounted access to – local cafés, restaurants, leisure centres, cinemas and theatres, would encourage a positive attitude towards the town centre rather than the negative one we often found.

The recession, together with increasing consumer resistance to 'sameness' in shopping centres, has sparked off a move back towards diversity. The famous Metro Centre in Gateshead, the largest self-contained out-of-town shopping mall in the UK to date, has put a ban on any further financial services companies taking shops because 'they don't give anything to the variety of the centre', and is seeking to include a post office, library and police station among new lettings. There is already a parish priest there. New local traders can start off by taking a barrow in the Metro Centre and, if successful, move into one of the proper shops. In Hounslow the Treaty Shopping Centre also contains a magnificent new public library which is as well used and popular as the Debenhams store next to it.

As part of the refurbishment of the Elephant and Castle shopping centre in south London, a new policy was adopted of not allowing any shopfronts to remain empty, as they gave the centre as a whole a negative image. Between lettings, shops are given over to community groups for exhibitions, classes and workshops. This has helped the centre to begin trading success-fully again. Lettings policy in retailing can also be regulated, as it was in Covent Garden where the GLC stipulated that there were to be no souvenir shops, no denim shops, that all shops had to remain open until 8 p.m., and rents were negotiated to ensure that a wide range of retailers could afford to come into the scheme. Recently, the new landlord of the main Covent Garden site, the Guardian Royal Exchange insurance company, has in-sisted on 'open market rents' which means that many of the specialist shops may go, to be replaced by the familiar multiple stores.

The privatization of leisure

It has been argued that another key factor in the decline of town-centre vitality has been the increased privatization of lei-sure and the growth of domestic entertainment. This has been put most tellingly by the sociologist, Laurie Taylor (1988), who has written: 'Today, the cinema and theatre have long since turned into the home video; the launderette and laundry into Ariston and Hotpoint; the library into Penguin and Pan; the concert hall into a compact disc.' The sheer visual evidence of the growth of video hire shops, the annual statistics published showing the degree of penetration of television in British households and the average number of hours it is watched each week (25.5 hours a week per average viewer), of the takeaway food and drink trade figures, all seem to attest to an irreversible trend towards the domestication of free time, a trend also supported by the major investment in homes and the continued growth of owner-occupation.

That trend has been also exacerbated by the growth of suburbanization, of urban 'growth by civic depletion' as Lewis Mumford (1945) called it, describing the proliferation of housing areas without any public amenities at all. A Conservative MP Sir Gerald Vaughan described the growth of suburban housing in and around Reading as follows: 'We have thousands of unhappy people who have moved into new houses on these huge estates. They find they have no proper schools, no shops, many of the roads are unmade and there is no proper health cover . . .'. The demand by developers to be allowed to build 'new villages' in South-East England has recently begun to be resisted by politicians and planners who fear for the green belt. Surely the real issue is to make existing towns and cities better places to live in?

We looked for, and found, evidence that pointed to contradictory patterns of free-time use. It was noted earlier that spending on physically active sports is slowly increasing, as is spending on eating out and going to the cinema. The growth of cinema admissions and the beginning of a downturn in video hire, the fact that half the eligible population visit a pub at least once a week, a quarter claim to eat out at least once a week, a quarter attend religious meetings, and 15 per cent of the population do voluntary work at least once a week, all suggested that people still led active lives, supported by statistics showing that there was no decline evident at all in participation in voluntary organizations, amateur music and drama clubs, and other self-organized groups. It can be argued that people still make effective choices in leisure and the majority still do go out quite frequently rather than stay at home 'glued to the television', as the popular stereotype has it.

The move from mass employment to smaller units, the growth of small business and self-employment, also contribute, we believe, to the possibilities of a renewed urban culture, as these forms of employment in themselves can regenerate urban areas through infill development, the transformation of redundant factories into managed workspaces, the growth of the services sector, bringing back into towns and cities new forms of production. The liberalization of 'use classes' in planning legislation can also be beneficial in mixing residential, light industry and retailing in or near town centres.

For the economic aspects of town-centre revitalization are of the greatest importance. Town-centre renewal can only come about if land-use planning is replaced by activity-based planning which works economically. We endorse the arguments made by Gerald Burke (1976) in a book on townscapes which summarizes the preconditions for a successful town or city:

A good-looking townscape is a product of a host of factors. These include: a workable structure of compatible land-use groupings, attractive layout and pride in the craftsmanship of buildings old and new, suitable densities of development, efficient public utilities services, convenient routes for vehicles and pedestrians, open space in appropriate amounts and locations, clearly defined urban–rural boundaries, space for expansion and, above all, a viable economy.

A programme for new, more localized urban economies, has already been outlined by the economist, Robin Murray (1991), in a study based on successful developments in Germany and Italy. Strengthening local economic circulations, of goods and services produced locally, is essential if towns and cities are to be shielded from the global effects of markets acting arbitrarily. The traditional 'one-industry' town cannot survive in the future as the fate of many of the shipbuilding, steel, fishing or mining towns in the UK has demonstrated. Flexible specialization in manufacturing, and the growth of service economies, puts local trading back on the agenda again. Ecological politics also provides the incentive for recycling, energy conservation, and a 'make-and-mend' approach to goods and services rather than deskilled mass production and consumption.

The research project embarked on was not looking for the ideal town or city or 'the best in Britain', nor was it looking for a way of providing a blueprint for urban perfection, a list of attributes which if all found together in one place would create a model city or utopian ideal. Every town we looked at had its strengths and weaknesses: some had breathtaking topographies, great industrial heritages, lively cosmopolitan populations; some had more than their fair share of planning disasters, high unemployment, over-cumbersome local government, and so on. Many had both. In the end the best way of describing what we hoped to find was that rather traditional concept of a 'working town': one that had a strong local economy, effective circulation of goods and services, a strong cultural identity based on past traditions but also a concern for the future, religious tolerance and civic open-mindedness, access to both urban and rural pleasures, intelligent and effective local government, and a respect for different lifestyles. In the chapters which follow, these attributes are examined in more detail.

2

Time and space in the modern town

Increasingly the values of commercial management are being seen as a central ingredient in shopping centre success, rather than being an extension of the local authority's role. Better a good 12 hours a day environment than a poor 24 hours.

McColl Architects & Designers, Market Vision *(1988)*

In Geneva that October he [Dickens] was physically ill, he wrote 'attributable, I have not the least doubt, to an absence of streets.'

F.S. Schwarzbach Dickens and the City *(1979)*

Historical determinants

Towns and cities are as they are as a result of different historical and cultural trajectories. We were aware of this all the time. It was visible in the layers of architectures, the incredible mixes and juxtapositions of old and new: neo-Gothic churches abutted by curtain-wall tower blocks, seventeenth-century coaching inns left stranded in the middle of a ring road, 1930s art deco cinemas converted into carpet warehouses, castle ruins surrounded by fax bureaux, prisons by car parks. No town was without this incredible confluence of styles and resonances. Statues, bandstands, great civic buildings and monuments to past ideals and aspirations now shared the town centres with monuments to the new international style of architecture and services:

25

hi-tech building societies, steel and glass gallerias, multiplex cinemas, fast food outlets and nightclubs. As Mumford (1945) expressed it:

Cities are a product of time. They are the moulds in which men's lifetimes have cooled and congealed, giving lasting shape, by way of art, to moments that would otherwise vanish with the living and leave no means of renewal or wider participation behind them.

This sense of the physical shape – of processes of decline and renewal in the townscape – as the backdrop to people's lives came across strongly wherever we talked to people. The familiarity with which people described certain streets, vanished buildings and districts or new developments, reminded us how strongly people both register and internalize the places in which they live. Still, for a significant proportion of any population, the town or city they are born in is the one that will shape their lives and become the stage-set of their hopes and aspirations; it will also register their sense of loss and missed opportunities. What the Italians call *campanilismo* (bell tower loyalty) can equally be found in Britain, except that it is more likely that the bell tower was demolished some years ago in order to build a new car park.

Privileging of time over space

In recent decades the process of change has accelerated, and the interests of urban space have been sacrificed to the interests of urban time. Time is now the element in which economies are made and unmade, into which markets expand and social life is stretched or contracted. The symbolic importance of the church bells or town-hall clock has long been superseded by the personal wristwatch and personal time. This is why the needs of car traffic have been prioritized over the needs of pedestrians, why retailing and development investment cycles are constantly lowered and that in order to provide returns on capital after three years rather than, say, ten years, buildings, interiors, façades and ownership change so frequently. It is why there are now at least four 'seasons' in the fashion shops each year rather than two. Everything depends on turnover. Many of the retail sheds going up on the perimeters of towns and cities only have a life of ten years; after that the investment will have been repaid and the buildings allowed to revert to dereliction. Land values have created a pressure to eradicate all 'waiting' space in towns; only high-turnover retailers can afford to be in the town centre and other services and facilities have been forced to the perimeter where rents and land are cheaper. The forces combine to deter the 'low-value' user from the town centre – the people with limited spending power who also play an important part in the life of the city, often to be found in the public library, in the parks and in the cheaper cafés on the edge of town. Yet paradoxically, in many cities such as Liverpool, Manchester and to a lesser extent, Swansea, there still remain large areas of derelict land in the city centre.

Time

Loss of public memory

One of the results of the speed and scale of urban redevelopment since the war, and the new patterns of multiple ownership of town-centre shops and services, has been the evident loss of 'public memory'. Time and again when asking people directions, or asking them to describe particular streets or districts, they would register a strong sense of confusion and frustration at their inability to 'name' the town or city in which they live. Most of the significant place-markers had disappeared or been changed. 'If you go down the High Street and turn left at – well it used to be the Coach and Horses but now it's Samantha's or Tiffany's – then keep right on past where the cinema used to be, left again where they've put the new car park which is a pity because that was where the wet fish shop and all those small shops were . . .'.

In Southend one High Street pub changed names twice in the year of the study; in many other towns pubs and bars were refitted and renamed every two years in line with some new brewery company theme. This real loss of local identities and place markers caused considerable stress to older people who felt that part of their own lives and identities had been taken away or destroyed. Pubs, department stores, tea-rooms, cinemas, street markets, local shops – all had disappeared in a welter of multiple investment in the immediate and short term retail markets.

The seven-to-eleven city

In arguing for greater flexibility in the use of town-centre space for more mixed uses, we also wanted both to note and encourage greater flexibility in the use of time. Quite simply the nine-to-five town centre no longer works except for shopping. Changes in lifestyle, in local patterns of work and living, in the massive participation of women in part-time work, and many other demographic and social factors, have produced a need for a different attitude to public culture and time. It may be that for retailers 'better a good 12 hours a day environment than a poor 24 hours', but urban life is about more than going shopping. There are leisure centres – such as Thamesdown's excellent Link centre in Swindon – open from 6 a.m. to 2 a.m., seven days a week, catering for all kinds of sports and leisure activity. Swansea's central Leisure Centre offers a very popular 'Swim and Breakfast' from 7.30 a.m. and at weekends the leisure pool is hired out for private parties which go on until the early hours of Sunday morning. In Woolwich such was the success of the Monday night women-only sessions at the Waterfront leisure centre, that this now happens on two nights a week; a specially lit car park attached to the centre helps make this a success with women. Feltham Sports Centre runs two women-only nights each week, when women have the run of the centre and can try anything they like.

It is interesting to note that in a recent policy statement on the cultural life of Milan, the City Council opened the report with a section drawing attention to the changing work patterns of women and the need to timetable cultural facilities accordingly.

Happy Hour

In response to evident attempts to meet changes in patterns of use, we developed the notion of 'time-shifting' to describe how activities might be better timed to coincide with people's needs and interests. The phrase comes from the media world, particularly that of video, where it is used to describe the pattern whereby people video a programme or film screened too early or too late for actual viewing, replaying it at a more convenient time. The pressures to do this are happening elsewhere, too. One of the most successful commercial initiatives in encouraging people to change their attitudes to time and usage was the pub 'happy hour', which came over from North America in the 1970s. Happy hour was a ruse to encourage people to use pubs in the early hours of the evening – when traditionally pubs have been at their quietest – by offering half-price drinks, usually spirits. Without condoning the practice, which many police argued was responsible for young people being drunk too early in the evening, it was a successful move in altering people's habits. British Rail, of course, does the same with its infinite variety of cheap fares designed to spread out the use of trains during the day and throughout the week. Pricing is a device for changing habits, and can be used for good and bad purposes. A number of cinemas charge half price on Mondays to encourage audiences who may tell their friends about the film, who in turn will attend later in the week.

In Newcastle restaurateurs have now picked up the message and they, too, offer substantial discounts on meals in the early evening; some have attributed the liveliness of Newcastle's night life to this expedient, which encourages town-centre workers to stay in town for the evening and have a cheap meal rather than go home and often not come back again. However, we also noted time changes in the opposite direction, for example in Woolwich, where all-day opening of the town-centre pubs has meant that the daily pattern of some local residents, if they are not in full-time work, is to come into town in the morning to shop, sign on, do various pieces of business, change library books, perhaps go swimming, then have a pub lunch, spend the early part of the afternoon in the pub and then go home for the rest of the day. This meant that in some pubs 'peak time' was now about 4 p.m. rather than 10 p.m.

Church on Wednesday

Not only was secular life adapting to changes in demographics and lifestyles. In Swansea the canon of the main town centre church, St Mary's, told us that he held most of his main services on Wednesday – four services in fact on that day – and as a result had regained the level of attendances he had lost when still sticking to Sunday (on which day, of course, he still holds services). The Wednesday programme of services was deliberately aimed at shoppers, town-centre workers, and had proved very successful, as it has done in Luton. Elsewhere we came across priests, vicars and other church workers using their churches for a variety of weekday purposes – meals for the homeless, playgroups, bring-and-buy sales, choral concerts, jazz concerts – apparently responding much more than many other organizations to new demands made by communities for space, resources and 'pastoral' space in the urban centre. Since many of the finest buildings left in town and city centres are church buildings, fruitful work could be done seeing how best they could be used as new centres of non-commercial activity in the new civic culture.

Opportunities and dangers of flexible time

Not only are the changes in employment patterns real and dramatic, the implications for urban policy must be so, too. By 1987, 45.7 per cent of all women were in full- or part-time work (Central Statistical Office 1989). Self-employment, both male and female, had grown considerably in the 1980s, as had unemployment. Many more jobs became part-time. This has produced not only a different time/space orientation to work – the morning and evening commuter rush to and from a single industrial or commercial estate is less evident than it was – but also a different attitude towards work. European surveys cited by the French sociologist, André Gorz (1989), have shown that a rapidly growing percentage of employees (about half the present number, as opposed to 29% in 1962), especially those under thirty (nearly two-thirds, as opposed to 39% in 1962) attach greater importance to their non-working activities than to their paid jobs.

Therefore, as work declines in symbolic importance in people's lives, so other activities will gain in importance – hobbies, personal relationships, community activities, watching television, crime. We know that fewer and fewer people are defining themselves by their job rather than by their hobbies or lifestyle: the latter are the new sources of personal identity. Flexitime at work and an interest in keeping fit, or doing voluntary work with the elderly, will produce pressures on all kinds of urban facilities to adapt to changing needs and timetables. At present policy and practice lag some way behind social change. It has often been said that in the past there was an inverse relationship between staffing and customer use in many sports centres. When there were most staff on duty there were fewest users, and when there were most users there were fewest staff. The staffing implications of providing leisure facilities – sports centres, libraries, museums and galleries, performances – when people most want them or are potentially capable of using them, are immense but they must be tackled.

For as we saw, it was precisely when for some people the library was most needed that is was closed: evenings and weekends. The same is true of many galleries and museums, and some sports facilities and centres. Floodlit pitches, for example, have been very popular for winter evening tennis and five-a-side football. Those providing for leisure and working in leisure must, by definition, be most available during other people's leisure time. With regard to flexibility of space, flexibility in time has to be a key ingredient of successful urban provision.

Sunday opening or a day for reflection?

This naturally raised the highly contentious issue of Sunday opening, when we talked to providers and policy-makers in towns about revitalizing urban centres. Late evening opening had not been successful in many shopping centres (though older people remembered shops and markets being open on Fridays and Saturdays until very late before the war, which had created the image or myth of a lost evening culture in many towns), but many retailers were keen to open on Sundays. Was what we were arguing for simply another day's shopping?

One argument on this subject suggests that Sunday opening should be restricted to 'reflective' or 'educational and participatory' activities, to distinguish Sunday from the rest of the week. This suggestion allowed for the opening of libraries, galleries, museums, sports centres, theatres, educational facilities, cafés and restaurants, possibly bookshops and record shops, but not for comparison shopping. Clearly based on a a major value judgement about 'worthwhile' or 'improving' activities, it nevertheless had a sense to it that other proposals have so far lacked.

Space

Mental maps

Each town is a different place to every individual who lives, works or visits there. Although there was a built form to each town available to all to see and negotiate, as well as a general consensus on the controversies which affected local social and political life, everybody we interviewed lived in a town or city of their own making. Everybody had their own 'mental maps', as Kevin Lynch (1960) has demonstrated. Every street, building, alley, department store or park, had different associations for different people. This was the subjective city, or the 'soft city' as Jonathan Raban (1981) described it when he argued that 'the soft city of illusion, myth, aspiration, nightmare, is as real, maybe more real, than the hard city one can locate in maps and statistics, in monographs on urban sociology and demography and architecture'.

Nowhere was this more apparent or more clearly demonstrated than in Woolwich, where our study luckily coincided with a study of women's attitudes to Woolwich town centre conducted by local planner, Wendy Davies, and Bridget Leach of Thames Polytechnic (Davies and Leach 1991). In the course of their study in 1990 they interviewed over 450 women about their attitudes to feelings of security in Woolwich town centre and found that every woman had her own individual list of 'secure' and 'unsafe' places in the town centre, naming particular bus stops, empty shop premises, even certain bushes or blind corners as places that caused anxiety. This study will be referred to later in greater detail, but we cannot underestimate the importance and relevance their work has for local planners and decision-makers in providing town and cities in which women can feel much safer than they do at present. The power of these mental maps to determine people's attitudes to going out, the degree to which people felt able or unable to move freely in their own town or city, was one of the most important findings of the project.

Compactness and sprawl

One of the greatest contributory factors in a sense of loss of local geography was the problem of sprawl. Retailing inched its way down suburban roads, popped up on a derelict out of town site, and housing drifted indeterminately into the surrounding rural hinterland. What had also disappeared in this development free-for-all was urban compactness, one of the most important features of any successful town or city. The Buchanan Report (Ministry of Transport 1963) had warned against this:

There are long-standing, well tried advantages in the principle of compactness for urban areas which are not to be lightly jettisoned in favour of the supposed advantages of dispersal. In a compact area, journey distances, including the all-important journeys to work and school, are kept to the minimum. The concentration of people makes it possible to provide a wider diversity of services, interests and contacts. There is a wider choice of housing, employment, schools, shops and recreational and cultural pursuits. It is easier in a compact society to maintain the secondary activities, such as restaurants, specialist shops and service industries which all too easily fail if there is not a large enough clientele close enough at hand.

These are what we called the 'critical mass' arguments for sustaining strong city centres with a diversity of uses. However, Patsy Healey (1990) has recently alerted planners to the fact that

---

It has become clear in the last twenty years that 'the market', to the extent that it can be isolated from the complex interrelations between political and economic decisions, is not reproducing the compact, contained and spatially ordered cities of either the economic models or the urban plans.

One of the main problems we had in the study was ascertaining where the town centre began and ended, and how one could correct the drift by default to urban sprawl and ribbon development.

Which town centre?

Where the town centre was and what it actually consisted of, was often a debatable issue, and had much to do with individual mental maps and personal associations. Many towns and cities have quite distinct retailing, commercial and civic areas all coexisting in the same square mile, but each with a highly different ambience. For many people the 'town centre' was the area where the town hall, art gallery, central library, law courts and other civic amenities were to be found – often the oldest buildings and the traditional centre. For some these were places of pride and architectural dignity, but for others these were places associated with bureaucracy, form-filling, births, marriages and deaths, and related officialdom, to be avoided at all costs. The retailing area had become the focus for town-centre activity, and many of the retail developers had cultivated this sense with the detailing of clock towers, fountains, small indoor applecart market squares in the new malls to encourage this belief that here was the new centre of town life and culture.

In Middlesbrough and Woolwich, Central Gardens and General Gordon Square are, respectively, landscaped town-centre sites linking mostly municipal facilities, but which feel sterile and unloved. There is an urgent need to think through the human aspects of developing new public spaces, and we have yet to see one which is really successful; Covent Garden is certainly brought to mind, although that is still primarily a retailing area. A problem evident in Basingstoke is that many of the office developments and company headquarters are so lavishly designed – with hanging gardens, atriums, private gardens – that the public realm seems downgraded in comparison.

Boundaries

Defining boundaries remains important even though it is un-likely that towns will need to be walled or moated to protect them from invading armies. We recommended in many of the towns that clear distinguishing features be developed to identify the town centre from the surrounding suburbs, whether in the form of signposts, pieces of public art, arches, gates, different lighting or other symbolic means. We even suggested a new civic ritual involving councillors 'beating the bounds' of the town or city centre once a year, ensuring that all signposts, town maps and other public facilities were in good order, free from graffiti and vandalism, and welcoming to users. Town-centre boundaries could also be used as a marking point for cheap bus fares, again identifying the town centre symbolically as a public domain with a special status.

Transitional spaces

Space – defensible, territorial, privileged, public or private – is now regarded as a much more complex ingredient in the urban realm than planners have traditionally understood. Space is an attitude of mind as much as a piece of geographical territory. Wars are fought over it; teenage gangs occasionally kill each other over it; neighbours come to blows over it. As outsiders to many towns, it was fascinating to observe the many resonances with which particular pieces of space were imbued. A single pedestrian subway could be the object of widespread and deep-est loathing; a small park and café just off the high street was talked about as if it were an unspoilt Eden. In between retailing

35

space, privileged to those with money to spend, commercial space for those who worked there or had transactions to undertake, and municipal space where local life was managed and ordered at a distance, there seemed to be fewer and fewer spaces where people could simply sit, meet, chat, watch the world go by, or review their life's work. The traditional café, tea-rooms or coffee house had been replaced by a fast food outlet, though some outposts of tradition survived.

Public libraries and galleries

One of the most important 'traditional' spaces where people can meet, sit or occasionally doze unharassed, are public libraries. If there is any hero or heroine to the story of modern urban culture it is the public library, one of the few spaces left in towns where one still sees a cross-section of all people going about their lives, all ages, conditions and classes, with little interference between them, and often with a purposefulness that was not seen elsewhere in the urban crowd. Parties of young schoolchildren were choosing books in the children's section, students studying in the reference library, older men picking their way through the daily newspapers, studious local historians beetling away in the local archives, dozens of others browsing and choosing books, records or videos. Some libraries had cafés, public telephones, art exhibitions, public notice-boards, talks and demonstrations. Most were well used, some were often full to overcrowding.

Yet there were problems. The poll tax (community charge) and other government restrictions on local spending had hit libraries hard. People complained about there being less choice of books, magazine subscriptions cancelled, shorter opening hours. In fact opening times seemed no longer suited to the way people wanted to use town centres, so that often libraries closed at exactly the time that most people were free to use them, particularly students doing homework or full-time workers – in the early evening. Another issue which emerged from talking to librarians was that the current policy of 'care in the community', involving the release of mental patients from institutional care, has resulted in some library staff having to spend time responding to the needs – and occasional dramas and incidents – of these patients who come to the library daily for somewhere to sit out of the cold. In one town we were told the situation had become distressing to staff as the 'core' activity of the library was being displaced by the need to enforce rules of behaviour and minister to quite serious personal needs.

Theatre bars: a safe haven for women

Theatres and art galleries also were important spaces for people, particularly women, to meet, especially if they had bars and cafés open during the day. In Liverpool many people we talked to knew the Everyman as a bistro as well as a theatre; in fact for some people the bistro is the main attraction as a meeting place as well as for its good food and lively atmosphere. In Liverpool also, the Walker Gallery café is another popular daytime venue. When we asked women in Swansea where they might meet another woman for a drink yet feel free of harassment, several immediately said the Grand Theatre bar/café. In Sheffield the Crucible foyer is heavily used on Saturdays by shoppers for meeting up and having something to eat or drink. In Preston the Harris Museum café is very popular. In fact in every town where the theatre had a public café or bar, this was always mentioned as a meeting place for women. It is interesting that it is the 'artistic' or 'cultural' ambience that creates this safe territory, free as it is from conventional brewery assumptions about spaces and drinking.

People-watching in department stores

There were few other havens in towns where tranquillity and conviviality overlapped. Where this was still likely was where there were traditional department stores with restaurants, and these often attracted a very distinct, mainly female, clientele. The restaurants in Binns, Middlesbrough, in David Evans in Swansea, in Keddies in Southend, even in Littlewoods in Woolwich, for example, had a quite different atmosphere from the street-level burger bars and cafés. Often they were in basements or on top floors and seemed deliberately to separate themselves out from the life of the high street, with trelliswork screens, potted plants, non-smoking areas, and a leisurely attitude towards customers, not clearing the table as soon as the cup of coffee was finished. Yet these department stores are themselves under threat: the Lewis group in the North of England went bankrupt at the beginning of 1991, and elsewhere stores have been converted into gallerias, franchising out the space to the familiar multiple outlets. People were very loyal to traditional stores: when Blacklers in Liverpool closed down, there was a palpable sense of the end of an era and both staff and customers wept on the last day of the closing-down sale. In Woolwich there was a consensus among people anxious for the future of the town centre that what was most needed was a 'good department store' to give the town centre a bit of solidity.

Parks and gardens

There were also parks, gardens and other open spaces with seating and shelter where people could meet or simply hang around and watch the world go by without spending any money. In Woolwich the large grassed central General Gordon Square island was very popular with local office workers, Polytechnic students and others in good weather at lunchtime, sitting out and having picnics or eating takeaway lunches, despite the bus fumes which wafted across it regularly. Complaints about drunks in the square were frequently heard, but, as the police pointed out, the busier the area is the less the drunks want to be there, for they, too, have a sense that they need a space they can call their own. In Middlesbrough the Victoria Gardens in front of the library are massively popular in good weather, yet there is no kiosk from which one could buy a coffee or an ice-cream. The same is true of Warrior Square Gardens immediately behind Southend High Street and of Castle Gardens in Swansea. Yet in St Paul's Square in Bedford there is a kiosk serving teas, coffees and snacks which is open all year round with seats and tables outside, and these are always used, even in winter. The argument that it is the British weather that prevents a café culture in Britain simply does not square with the statistics: the average rainfall in Paris is 566 mm and in London 581 mm. Many northern European towns and cities with similar or worse weather conditions sustain a culture of sitting outside.

A change of attitude is needed if town-centre public spaces

are to work well, for at present they are often popular despite the facilities rather than because of them. Traditional attitudes mean that 'maintaining' a town park means cutting the grass, bedding the roses and emptying the litter bins; what it has yet to mean is providing good toilets, a choice of light refreshments, children's activities, occasional live music or theatre, and turning the space into an occasional 'urban stage'. So often we noticed that where there was town-centre seating it was designed so that people sat back to back, or in a circle looking out, rather than creating seating arrangements where people could sit and talk in groups or circles, face to face.

There is no reason why the major retailers should not provide a contribution to the funding of these activities if the town centre is to retain its appeal to all sections of the community and remain a place where people want to be. The fact that the very newest of the retail developments also incorporate leisure and entertainment is proof of the understanding that retailing alone cannot sustain lively town centres. Technological development means that it is now possible quickly to erect giant portable video screens in open spaces, to relay operas, musicals, football matches, and various other kinds of programming which would have a wide appeal. The immense success of the occasional outside relays, from Covent Garden Opera House to crowds in the square outside, attests to the popularity of these more public forms of free entertainment. There should be more.

Programmes or buildings?

Many of the questions related to the dullness and lack of vitality in urban public spaces lead back to the problem of how so much of arts and entertainment spending is essentially building-based rather than activity-based. Councils spend considerable amounts of money each year maintaining theatres, concert halls, civic halls, assembly rooms, galleries and museums, often spending more on maintenance costs than they do putting on exhibitions, events or programmes inside them. One senior leisure officer told us that his council spent more each year painting the outside of the art gallery than they did on putting exhibitions inside it. We were convinced that in future much greater flexibility will be needed in putting on arts programmes if local civic culture is to survive and respond to new cultural changes rather than atrophy or fight a rearguard action to defend a minority programme of mainstream (and often second-rate commercial) theatre and gallery space against all other forms of cultural participation and enjoyment. The attendance figures at some galleries, museums and theatres simply did not warrant the amount they cost the local authorities, when so much else that was lively and popular locally was unsupported, particularly that involving young people or ethnic minorities.

This issue is now the subject of a report by the Audit Commission (1991) which recommends radical reappraisal of local government policy and spending on arts and entertainments to make it more effective and to reach more people. The use of portable venues for theatre, musical concerts and ballet which may only secure full audience on ten occasions a year makes more sense than building new large venues and then worrying about filling them for the other 340 days and nights. We were told in one town that local artists preferred to exhibit in the main library rather than in the art gallery, as more people saw their work and they sold more at the library. In another town an Asian dance company only had an audience of twenty in the town theatre but attracted an audience of a hundred when invited to perform in a local dance and fitness studio. Many touring theatre companies prefer to go to schools rather than theatres; photographic exhibitions have had bigger audiences in shopping centres than in theatre foyers; live bands have had bigger audiences at free summer concerts in the park than at a dozen pub gigs. Creating new and exciting relationships between audiences and spaces deserves serious consideration in cultural planning, and cannot simply be resolved by voting for extra bricks and mortar or refurbishing redundant listed buildings in the wrong part of town.

The street

Insufficient attention has been paid in recent years to defining the qualities of successful streets as key public spaces in the urban context. Le Corbusier (in Middleton 1987) must take some of the blame for arguing in the 1920s that 'We must kill the street. We shall truly enter into modern town planning only after we have accepted this preliminary determination.' Le Corbusier was arguing no doubt as a rationalist in an era in which religion seemed in decline, and the days of the religious street procession – for Mumford the key to the 'visible city' – were clearly numbered. But streets have served other ritualistic functions – for demonstrations, flag-day marches, carnivals and even motorcades – and can continue to do so. We were struck by a remark made to us by a town-centre priest asked to give evidence of possible civic decline: 'there are no big funerals in Middlesbrough any more'.

Buchanan (1988) also saw the unique importance of the street to urban life when he argued:

It is often said that streets are for the passage of traffic only, and although this may be a sound legal view it has obscured the fact that streets perform other functions, some of them vital. They give access to buildings, they provide an outlook from buildings, they give light and air, they are the setting for architecture, and they are the backbone of the everyday surroundings for many people.

Much of the inspiration for Dickens's novels came from the nineteenth-century street, and when ill in Geneva he admitted that his debilitation was due to 'an absence of streets'. Over-romantic, perhaps, in an era of pedestrianized town centres and muzak-filled shopping malls, but there is still a chance that the unexpected will happen on a street, that people will meet, stop and gossip, renew acquaintances with long-lost friends 'bumped into' accidentally – that is less likely to happen in a suburban street, workplace or institutional setting. Being 'street-wise' or having 'street credibility' is still a much prized virtue among the young, and 'street culture' survives as strongly as ever within youth, music and fashion cultures.

Walking and promenading

We frequently encountered the argument that the under-developed café and open air culture of Britain was due to the

41

weather and we repeatedly argued against this pervasive myth or explanation. As Mark Girouard (1990) reminded us, the social promenade was actually invented in Britain and the landscaping of urban walks in Britain was admired throughout Europe:

The English have lost the habit of social walking, once as common in Britain as the *passeggiatas* of Continental Europe. But in the eighteenth century malls, parades, walks, promenades or esplanades were the outdoor counterpart of assembly rooms, the places where polite society came 'to see or be seen'.

In fact this judgement is premature. In Southend the seafront to the west of Southend pier is thronged with walkers on summer evenings and at weekends throughout the year, in couples, in family groups and other combinations. The Southend scene is genuine European social promenading, and may owe some of its survival to the strong Jewish community in the town who are among the most dedicated promenaders. Swansea's new Maritime Quarter is beginning to develop something of that same promenading culture. Many other European countries, with climates similar to if not harsher than that of Britain, maintain a much stronger public café culture, and as the architect, Deborah Brookman (1990), has argued: 'The defeatist argument that a public culture is not possible in the north of Europe as a result of the weather seems inappropriate since the truly public parks of London are well frequented and loved.'

In other towns, the streets are at times overflowing with people, but this mainly now takes the form of youth pub and club visiting in the evenings and at weekends, where in many towns there is a distinct 'fashion circuit' of city-centre pubs that have each to be visited in turn. At the weekend in Swansea there are often as many as 5000 young people on the streets in the early hours of the morning after the clubs have closed; in Middlesbrough and Preston proportionately large numbers are also involved. The 'Friday night millionaires', local people call them. Some politicians, though uneasy with the drinking and occasional violence, have at least welcomed the fact that young people are coming into the town centre again, and hope that as they get older they will retain this habit.

Street life is essentially about short journeys. The more interesting the activities in a street the longer the journey will take and the less it will become a 'traffic movement', as the planners might call it. Yet as Mayer Hillman and Anne Whalley (1979) have suggested, it is an accepted view that long journeys are always more important than short ones. Why? Surely the escorting of children to school, the daily shopping trip and morning coffee with friends that many pensioners make, the window shopping, the business transaction conducted in the street, are all as socially and even economically important as the motorway commuter journey? 'Indeed,' argues Judy Hillman (1990) in a recent and invaluable defence of street culture, 'people going about their business is one of the keys to the successful street'.

Judy Hillman argues for serious rethinking about the large amount of unnecessary street furniture which has accumulated in British streets, ostensibly in the interest of pedestrians – including crush barriers, planters, litter bins, bollards, traffic signposts, parking meters, street lights – much of which could have been designed to be suspended from above, attached to walls, or in other ways detached from the actual pavements, leaving them free to be walked upon without hindrance. Her argument is that clean, well-serviced streets make business sense, bringing life back into towns and encouraging business diversity.

However, from other quarters the 'freedom of the streets' is under serious scrutiny. In response to street crime, shoplifting and other town-centre problems, more authoritarian responses have been argued. Closed-circuit television monitoring of the high street has been suggested in a number of British town centres, and, even more radical, the 'privatization' of streets. In May 1989 the Adam Smith Institute published a study advocating precisely this, though in fairness it was arguing only about the possible privatization of residential streets rather than town-centre thoroughfares. But even the suggestion of more private spaces in towns and cities seems to be going in the wrong direction, for, as we have seen, some town centres are now privatized *de facto* by the degree to which private shopping malls have commandeered the main urban centres with their nine-to-six opening hours. In our understanding of what is needed to revitalize urban life, safety and security will be best accomplished through the presence of more people on the streets involved in a diversity of activities – 'natural surveillance', as it has been called – rather than through fewer people and more locked gates, shuttered precincts and closed-circuit camera surveillance.

Ribbons and lines rather than circles and squares

The very form of recent urban development has taken an anti-pedestrian stance in its preference for ribbons and lines rather than circles and squares. Again, Le Corbusier's dictum that the straight line is always superior to the curve may have something to do with the spatial development of the modern town or city. The market square of the medieval town or city has been replaced by the linear high street or ribbon development leading from the town centre into the suburbs. Most of Southend's wide and actually very good range of restaurants are strung out along five or six kilometres of the London Road leading from Southend Victoria Circus to Leigh; Middlesbrough's restaurant area is stretched out along Linthorpe Road. In Woolwich there are some quite good restaurants, but they are completely isolated from each other. There is no sense here of the restaurant 'quarter' or district of many other European towns where people wander around looking at display menus before choosing – and with the opportunity of meeting friends. In the towns we looked at, it was more the case of park the car outside, go in to eat, and then go home again.

Districts and quarters

Visualizing and mapping town centres as quarters, and developing planning briefs from that process might be a new way forward. Although a mixture of residential, retail, entertainment and light industrial use in town centres remains the priority, some segmentation may be necessary in order to achieve more highly localized identities and microeconomies. For it certainly does help if most restaurants are in the same area, or that most entertainment and leisure facilities are linked. Both Liverpool's and Manchester's Chinatowns are important evening districts and economies; in Swansea the development of the Maritime Quarter based around the Council's own early development of a leisure centre there and subsequently developed around other leisure interests and attractions – the Museum, the Dylan Thomas Theatre, the Swansea Craft Workshops, a number of pubs and restaurants, the marina itself, with everything enhanced by an ambitious programme of public art – has genuinely created a new city district with a strong identity of its own. Albert Dock in Liverpool is another case in point. Both Gloucester and Preston are developing interesting dockside quarters which mix residential accommodation, retailing and leisure facilities.

Markets and fairs

The town square was traditionally the site of the regular open market where local traders could sell their produce or goods. Where such street markets still existed they were greatly valued by local people not only because of the cheapness of the products or the range of fresh produce, but also because they had 'atmosphere', the stalls were run by 'characters', often by families who had been trading for generations. But they were also spaces where ethnic minority traders could set up shop. In Woolwich the daily street market, everyone agreed, provided the 'heart' of the town centre. In Preston fierce (successful) battles were waged to prevent the relocation of the town's traditional covered market; and in addition to the market there are now regular car-boot sales in the town centre on Tuesdays and Thursdays. In Swansea people talked about the covered market as being the last remaining link with 'the old Swansea town centre'. Street markets and covered markets were regarded as popular space, still owned by local people. Shopping centres were regarded as belonging to 'them', no matter how benign or attractive the shops or facilities.

Pedestrianization

All of the towns had pedestrianized areas in the town or city centre. Southend High Street was one of the first in the country. The consensus was that pedestrianization had been highly successful, both for traders and shoppers – though there were some dissenting voices, often quite pronounced. The drawbacks to pedestrianization, it was claimed, came at night when pedestrianized areas became almost completely deserted; previously car traffic had been an important contribution to a feeling of passing surveillance and safety. In Southend this was often given as the main explanation as to why the town centre had become a feared and unliked place at night. There are good reasons for believing that dual (though highly regulated) use of pedestrian areas at night by both cars and people should be developed; there are many examples in North America and in Europe of controlled car traffic in areas where pedestrians retain priority, and this is the scheme now proposed in Swansea: 'pedestrian priority' in the town centre rather than wholesale pedestrianization.

Offices right down to the ground

What has to be resisted at all costs in town centres is the creation of blank walls, dark glass frontages, shopfront services which offer nothing visually to the town centre and have only an instrumental function in the high street or shopping mall. Women in particular fear empty shop windows and doorways as much as the more obvious visual affronts such as graffiti or strident advertising hoardings. Where there is commercial accommodation in town centres it should offer retailing or other interactive functions or facilities at ground-floor level. As Richard Rogers has complained about certain London developments: 'There are offices right down to the ground on major thoroughfares. That means that the public has lost the public realm' (Campbell 1989). In Woolwich the local council has admirably sited some of its key local services in shopfront locations in the main town centre, but because these are often curtained or employ some other means of making them blind to the street, the effect is disastrous. In Basingstoke the outer walls of the main shopping centre present a vast brick cliff face to people in surrounding streets; in Southend the new shopping centre, the Royals, built at the southern end of the High Street on the main site overlooking the pier and estuary, presents a blank face to the sea, so that inside the people sitting in the Food Court remain unaware of the potential view that could have been available to them if the architect or developer had not made such an extraordinary choice. In France and other countries it is not unusual for banking and insurance services to be provided at first-floor level, leaving ground-floor sites for genuine retailing. At the Elephant and Castle shopping centre it was realized that empty shop premises created an atmosphere of decline and dereliction, and so as soon as shops are vacated they are offered to community groups or new businesses on short lets simply in order to create a sense of occupation and activity.

Accommodation in the town centre

In Liverpool it was clear that rents were so high in the main town centre that it was cheaper for the stores to leave the rooms above the ground floor empty, and to take away all stairways inside to create more ground-floor space for retailing. The result of this was, as in many other towns, that rooms, premises, offices and residential accommodation above shops were left empty, because their usage would interfere in some way with the activities at ground-floor level. The planning department in Swansea has estimated that there is over 150,000 square feet of vacant upper floorspace in two main streets, High Street and Wind Street. If safety issues prevent people from coming into town centres at night, then having more people living in town-centre accommodation can only improve matters. There is now an organized campaign to encourage the use of Swansea High Street premises for accommodation and naturally we supported this and recommended involvement in the campaign in the towns we studied. The lesson had already been learnt in a number of the towns we looked at, for certainly Middlesbrough, Preston and Swansea all had housing programmes that bought back residential accommodation in or near the town centre, in some cases for elderly people who simply did not want to be banished in the last years of their lives to the suburban hinterlands.

Electronic time and space

Time and space have been stretched, too, in the electronic media. It is still the case that few young black people come into Liverpool city centre as a rule; their most important form of public space and time is Toxteth Community Radio (TCR) which gives them freedom of the airwaves to play the music they like, discuss the issues of importance to their community, and directly address their peers and many others in their own homes. Local and community radio has still to find a developed role in Britain (compared to North America or Australia, for example), and mostly we found indifference to both BBC and independent local radio stations. Where there was excitement and interest it was around pirate stations or very strong local personalities on mainstream local radio, such as the DJ Roger Hill in Liverpool. As part of the research for *Out of Hours*, a late-night radio phone-in was organized on Piccadilly Gold station in Manchester, and there were dozens of callers who wanted to discuss the city centre until 2 a.m. when the show finished.

The wired city

Technologists and futurologists have sometimes argued that the future of towns and cities is as 'teletopias', 'telecommunities' or 'wired cities': geographical areas linked by various interactive services such as cable, video, telecoms, creating new communities of interest or 'neighbourhoods without propinquity' (Mulgan 1989). Britain lags behind many other countries in developing these new media, and, as Geoff Mulgan (1989) has pointed out:

Yet the long term promise of the wired cities experiments is undeniable. In France, nearly 200 cities now offer a wide range of information, often providing possibilities for interaction, such as polls on local issues, and systems for finding information about housing opportunities or making a reservation at a local municipal theatre. The better ones have tried to create a system of two-way communication rather than simply dumping propaganda on an inert citizen. Grenoble has developed probably the most sophisticated set of tools for communicating with its citizens, an approach which has been vindicated by record turnouts for local referenda on such issues as tram policies.

What the wired city does best is not to keep people imprisoned in their houses, flats and rooms, but provide them with the information, contacts, networks and programmes to enable them to use the town or city more effectively. It creates audiences and publics in advance of the event or performance; it short-circuits urban time and space to potentially link people up in anticipation of actual city use and enjoyment. The wired city is not the enemy of the working city or town but its new intellectual and informational framework. These challenges are only just beginning to present themselves in British towns and cities.

3

Safety in numbers: towards women-friendly cities

The first thing to understand is that the public peace — the sidewalk and street peace — of cities is not kept primarily by the police, necessary as police are. It is kept primarily by an intricate, almost unconscious, network of voluntary controls and standards among the people themselves, and enforced by the people themselves . . . No number of police can enforce [this peace] where the normal, casual enforcement of it has broken down.

Jane Jacobs, The Death and Life of Great American Cities *(1964)*

Law and order paradigm

In the 1970s questions of town-centre decline were mostly associated with planning disasters, particularly ring roads, brutalistic car parks and first-generation roughcast concrete shopping centres. In the 1980s the issue of urban malaise came to be seen essentially as a problem of law and order, of unsafe cities and town centres, pub violence, street riots, and women afraid to go out at night for fear of mugging, rape or murder. The interstices of the new or comprehensively redeveloped urban form became peopled with popular fears and nightmares. The 'Yorkshire Ripper' murders cast a terrible shadow over urban night life, not just in Leeds but throughout northern Britain. Time and again people were warned by the police and other authorities that the best hope for personal safety lay in staying at home, certainly for women. Going out at night became regarded less as a sign of well-being than as a sign of foolhardiness or even irresponsibility.

Women victims of all kinds of horrific crime were judged somehow to be partly culpable or responsible for what had happened to them, simply by being in the wrong place at the wrong time, as Gill Valentine (1989) has clearly shown. A national MORI survey in 1987 (in Atkins 1989) reported that 40 per cent of respondents feared going out at night, a figure rising to 64 per cent among women. In every town we studied, this 'moral panic' about the town centre having become a place of fear and violent crime was a widespread local perception. Most local newspapers had at some time or other splashed town-centre violence and drunken mayhem across the front pages, sometimes with monotonous regularity. If people had not been worried about going out at night until they read the papers, they certainly were afterwards. However, when we came to conduct our study, a backlash against irresponsible local press reporting and scaremongering had set in, particularly among the police, and everywhere the new cliché was to be heard that 'it's not crime that keeps people indoors these days, but the fear of crime'. The police were now hurriedly trying to reassure people that life really was not so dangerous after all.

Looking for evidence: is crime more perceived than real?

The extent to which urban criminality, perceived and real, had become a major issue in people's lives, emerged in the two Islington Crime Surveys (Crawford *et al.* 1990) conducted by Professor Jock Young and colleagues at Middlesex Polytechnic in 1985 and 1988, funded by the Economic and Social Research Council and cited everywhere. In the Islington survey it emerged that even in the three years between the first and second reports residents not only grew more worried about crime but also saw themselves surrounded by dirty streets, graffiti, vandalism, verbal abuse, dog excrement and other attributes of urban decline which they associated as part and parcel of a 'criminal environment'. This close relation between physical disrepair and fear of going out also emerged in our study, particularly in Manchester where a group of middle-aged working-class women interviewed were affronted by the dereliction of the environment and regarded it almost as a personal insult to them.

On almost every criminal issue people perceived the situation to have remained unchanged or in many cases worsened – in terms of street robbery, domestic burglary, fights and street disturbances, vandalism, sexual assaults on women, heroin use, domestic violence, sexual abuse of children, physical cruelty towards children, racial attacks and people being afraid to go out by themselves after dark. Only with regard to prostitution did people perceive there to have been an improvement (that is, decline in visible activity). A picture emerged of a metropolitan residential community living in fear. Even at home people did not feel safe, with 49 per cent of women and 23 per cent of men claiming sometimes to feel unsafe indoors.

Yet with regard to going out the situation was even worse. Some 73 per cent of women and 27 per cent of men felt worried about going out alone after dark. As many as 68 per cent of women under 25 took some sort of avoidance action at night through fear of crime, avoiding certain streets, carrying items that could be used as weapons of self-defence. Some 43 per cent of women claimed to avoid public transport at night for fear of crime. These findings coincided with and confirmed work then being done in Islington in 1987 by Comedia on the take-up of arts provision in the borough. One of the key findings from a sample of 500 residents was that what deterred many women and elderly people from going out to the cinema, bingo, theatre, live music pubs and other forms of entertainment was sheer fear of going out alone or using public transport, a fact hitherto little taken into account by arts providers.

When asked which crimes they thought the police ought to pay more attention to, in the Islington Crime Survey (Crawford *et al.* 1990), 'sexual assaults on women' and 'street robbery with violence' were the most mentioned priorities. The survey is now widely quoted as being one of the most comprehensive pictures of urban fears of crime to date, and although the inner-city London Borough of Islington is by no means representative of mainstream British life, enough commentators from other places in Britain found echoes of these findings where they lived and worked.

Home Office Safer Cities Project: the cost of crime

The Home Office Safer Cities Project was launched in 1988 in response to increasing public concern about rising crime, and targeted 20 British cities for research into patterns and perceptions of urban crime. It also followed on from what was regarded as a successful Community Programme initiative – the '5 Towns' project – which had not only investigated crime in Bolton, North Tyneside, Croydon, Swansea and Wellingborough, but also established crime prevention programmes which had, for the length of the experiment at least, reduced crime on urban housing estates where the projects had mostly been based. However, the '5 Towns' project had revealed the extent to which fear of crime had deterred people from using the town centre. In Croydon two-thirds of those responding to a residential survey gave fear of crime as their reason for avoiding the town centre at night; in Wellingborough 41 per cent of people interviewed said they avoided the town centre at night for the same reason.

The Nottingham Safer Cities Project concentrated on community safety in the town centre, and a Steering Group report published in 1990 makes salutary reading for those concerned with the extent to which crime and the use of the city at night now intersect so damagingly. A commissioned public opinion survey in Nottingham found that: a substantial proportion of respondents always or usually avoided the city centre after dark; of those respondents using the city centre after dark, 45 per cent felt very unsafe or fairly unsafe; and between them respondents mentioned 27 specific places in Nottingham city centre that they would avoid. Using these figures it was estimated that popular abandonment of the city centre after dark for fear of crime, meant the loss of some £12 million turnover and 442 job opportunities in Nottingham.

Of the recommendations which followed from this report, two areas are worth highlighting. The first is the importance in future of considering, in the words of the report, 'the safety of people and property together rather than separately', citing the many incidences where high fences and walls, or blocked-off doors and shuttered windows, while possibly deterring criminals, have in fact made places feel more threatening for people using them. The second key issue concerns the safety of public transport – as we are aware, very much the province of women and the elderly – and here the report regrets the demise of the bus conductor and explores the prospect of women-only bus schemes and other aspects of women's 'safe transport schemes' already operating in Bradford, Bristol and a number of London boroughs. Finally, it seems, even government agencies have recognized gender as a crucial factor in urban policy.

The fact that men and women have completely different experiences of urban life was also revealed in a report published in 1990 from the Edinburgh District Council's Women's Committee, which sought to amend or modify the external image of Edinburgh as having the best quality of life of most towns or cities in Britain, by pointing out that this was a one-sided truth only. For women domestic, social and civic life in the city was still far from ideal. Dirty streets, poor bus services, inadequate street lighting, sexual harassment in the city centre, and, most importantly of all, lack of childcare facilities, all contributed to women feeling disenfranchised from Edinburgh's internationally admired cultural life.

Such was the growing concern about women's safety in the latter part of the 1980s that women's magazines, such as *Company*, ran their own campaigns on the issue. The 'Safe Company' campaign, which was running while we were conducting our own studies, was a monthly page in the magazine which highlighted examples of good practice in supporting women in urban environments, and published suggestions and case studies from women readers as to how they had started to tackle the question of safety on the streets in Britain. It even awarded 'Safe Company Certificates' to local councils which had run successful schemes including releasing women workers for self-defence classes during working hours, improving taxi-licensing safeguards and encouraging taxi-drivers to see women to their doors, improving street lighting, establishing 'hail-and-ride' bus services in the evening so that women did not have to stand at deserted bus stops. It was one of the most successful magazine campaigns of the 1980s, and demonstrated how important and urgent the issue had become.

Town-centre crime

Local newspapers and the climate of fear

In all the towns we looked at many of the people we talked to largely attributed the local 'climate of fear' to sensationalist reporting in the local press. We were shown many front-page headlines which turned small-scale local youth drinking sprees into apocalyptic scenarios of gang warfare, indiscriminate violence and the collapse of law and order. One local newspaper described Gloucester as 'thug city'. In Middlesbrough, Preston, Swansea and Southend, the perceived town-centre drink culture was one of the main issues which prompted the councils to participate in the *Out of Hours* study (Comedia 1991). Yet when we spent evenings visiting the pubs and clubs in these towns, or accompanying the police on a late evening patrol in a police car, what we mostly saw were young people being sick in the gutter and looking helpless, bewildered and somewhat ill. There was often a lot of shouting and swearing, which was intimidating in its own way, but, as with most other crime, such violence as there was was directed at other young people in the immediate group rather than at strangers or passers-by.

But the newspaper reporting had been effective. People often referred to reports in the newspaper rather than direct experience to justify their decision to stop going into the town-centre at night. Older, usually male and middle-aged, journalists rhapsodized about the town-centre nightlife they remembered fondly from their youth, but which they now saw as excluding them and therefore to be deplored. As always, the local newspapers responded to events, amplified them, and created yet another self-fulfilling prophecy. The social and economic costs of a continual barrage of bad publicity are immeasurable.

More crime committed during daytime

In reality, of course, most town- or city-centre crime is daytime crime. Over 25 per cent of city centre crime in Nottingham was shop theft, with car theft and theft from motor vehicles (predominantly in the daytime) accounting for another 25 per cent. Sexual offences accounted for only 0.3 per cent of the total reported crime in the city centre (however, it should be remembered that it has been estimated that only 8 per cent of sexual offences are ever reported). In Croydon 61 per cent of town-centre crimes were car crimes, mostly occurring in two particular town-centre car parks. Shoplifting and stealing from cars in car parks are the main forms of town-centre crime and are daytime phenomena. In Southend the police told us that they had more trouble with young people during the day than at night. However, most daytime crimes are crimes of property rather than crimes against the person. The police view in Basingstoke was that crime spread out from the town centre as the evening wore on, and was more likely to take the form of 'domestics' later on at night after a night out by one or both parties.

Women workers and shoppers in town centres

During daytime, the majority of people in town centres are likely to be women – as shop workers and as shoppers. As was noted in the Swansea study, female full- and part-time workers accounted for 65.7 per cent of town-centre shop workers, compared with 25.1 per cent male workers (the 9.0 per cent unaccounted for were casual workers). Nationally, of 1,950,000 retail employees in the sector as a whole, 660,000 (34 per cent) are male and 1,290,000 (66 per cent) female. Figures for the proportion of women to men as town-centre shoppers we found impossible to locate, but visual impressions alone (and traditional gender roles) confirm the overwhelming presence of women as shoppers in most town centres during the day. Yet town centres remain planned, managed and policed by men. Only men, we were told on a number of occasions, would plan shopping centres without toilets, childcare facilities or seats. Only men would give priority to car parking (capital costs of providing a single space are currently estimated at between £4,000 and £10,000 per bay) over play areas, crèches, or dial-a-ride bus services for the elderly.

Women on business

Women now make up 45 per cent of the workforce, with nearly 2 million more joining the labour force since 1983. The number of self-employed women has doubled since 1979. The government expects women to account for more than 90 per cent of labour-force growth over the next decade. Increasingly, women are moving not just into part-time unskilled jobs (though many, of course, are) but also into positions of executive responsibility and status. Yet again, both public and private sectors have been slow to adapt to these new patterns of employment and urban usage.

Business women, like their male counterparts, will travel to and stay in other towns and cities on business, yet facilities for them to do so remain underdeveloped and in some places non-existent. In some places no thought at all has gone into planning for these new women's roles. A survey of business women travelling alone found that 65 per cent were 'extremely dissatisfied' with services offered by leading hotel chains, and a scheme to enable unaccompanied women travellers to meet and dine with each other is now in operation. We always asked, as a matter of course, where a single female stranger to a town might arrange to meet a professional colleague in the evening. Most people we asked found it difficult to think of somewhere immediately. Most pubs were immediately dismissed out of hand, most cafés or restaurants assumed to be closed, and such hotels as there were were often at some distance from the town centre. Eventually there was usually a consensus that there might be just one wine bar, hotel lobby or theatre bar in any town where the presence of a single woman waiting would be accepted as a matter of course. There clearly should be more.

Women in Woolwich

In Woolwich the *Out of Hours* study coincided with a detailed survey of women's attitudes to the town centre conducted by

57

local Council planner Wendy Davies and Dr Bridget Leach of Thames Polytechnic. Their team interviewed 420 women in one week in June 1990 in the town centre and found that 65 per cent of women felt afraid at night, and a surprising 36 per cent felt afraid during the day. The main daytime fear was mugging or robbery and the main night-time fear was attack, assault or rape. Younger women were able to be more specific about what they feared, but older women spoke about a 'nameless' fear associated with going out at night. The environmental factors which made women feel most unsafe were the sight of empty shops, dense shrubbery in and around the town centre, longer pub opening hours, and the high number of soldiers in the town (Woolwich is a garrison town). Sixty-three per cent of the women interviewed used buses much of the time and 34 per cent walked to the town centre. Particular bus stops were frequently mentioned as a cause for concern, as were certain pedestrian underpasses and footways. Some 77% of those interviewed took some form of action to make themselves feel safer when going out at night, such as choosing routes in advance, avoiding certain places, carrying something that could be used as a weapon, or being ready to run. When asked what would make them feel safer, lighting and policing were the factors most often mentioned; having more people around was also mentioned a lot but with the qualification that 'more people' did not include 'gangs' of young males. The survey is perhaps the most exhaustive study of women's attitudes to town-centre usage we have, and its findings provide lessons for all kinds of provision in future. What was also instructive about the survey was the degree to which each individual woman interviewed had constructed her own 'mental map' of the town centre, down to mentioning particular shop doorways, bushes, bus stops and alleyways which constituted a potential threat or danger to her.

Women and transport

Public transport, as we have seen, is a major issue of concern to women. However, in many towns the 'public' part of the transport provision no longer seemed meaningful. Deregulation had often produced a decline in off-peak bus services, older and dirtier buses and trains, and a complete severance with local authorities on wider questions of policy. As Stephen Atkins (1989) has written: 'It should also be recognised that many public-transport operations are more than simply an economic enterprise. They provide an important component of the spatial and social structure of the community.' Beyond bus transport, there were other aspects of urban transport policy that emerged as requiring new thinking.

Taxis

Where they can afford them – and in some towns taxi fares now seem level with bus fares, particularly if two people are travelling together – women will use taxis. But do they know what they are getting if they call for a minicab or a taxi to collect them from home, or if they call one from a restaurant or station? There is no guarantee that minicab drivers have undergone any form of screening whatsoever – for driving ability, criminal record, or even local knowledge of geography or routine destinations. Some kind of thorough regulation of the minicab business seems essential. Minicab offices were often cited as places to be avoided in the list of women's fears.

Licensed taxis offer a better deal, and we believe there are grounds for enhancing the value of local taxi services to the urban economy by additional forms of training and other common services. Taxi drivers could be encouraged to give advice on evening entertainment available in towns; in Chicago taxi drivers who have trained to be 'cultural guides' are allowed to charge higher fares. Taxi drivers can be trained to be more sensitive to the apprehensions of women passengers, escorting them to the door of their homes or other destination. And, of course, more women could be encouraged to train as taxi drivers – the setting up of women-only taxi companies has already happened in some places. In Middlesbrough the Students' Union runs a women-only minibus service after dances and discos, and the Women's Officer at the Students' Union there told us that a number of women students would not come to these events unless this service was provided afterwards.

Sex offences on trains

So worrying were the findings of a survey undertaken by British Transport Police into passenger safety fears on London commuter trains, that it was decided to suppress the report in 1989 until leaked copies became available to the press. Some 2,000 questionnaires were handed out to travellers at Liverpool Street and Fenchurch Street stations in October 1988; 922 were returned, 81 per cent of them from women. More than 30 per cent of the respondents claimed to have witnessed serious fights or assaults in the previous 12 months, but only 6 per cent had reported them, largely they claimed because of lack of staff to report them to. The report itself admitted: 'The over-riding impression from the replies received is that some women feel extremely vulnerable travelling after the evening rush hour, whether because of fears of indecency offences or a general discomfort when near drunks.' The main complaints, in descending order of frequency were: drunkenness and disorder; assault and indecency; graffiti and vandalism; theft and damage in car parks; and smoking in non-smoking compartments.

The following year the British Transport Police annual report noted that the number of sex offences on BR services had increased by 61 per cent, and on London Underground services by 46 per cent. There is clearly a major problem of women's security on BR services, and little evidence that it is being addressed. In Woolwich the local commuter train service is notorious among women for attacks, and BR has only recently dropped single compartment (rather than through-compartment) trains after intense local pressure.

London Underground seems to have made a calculated decision to cut costs and staff and to be prepared to lose women travellers in the evening, according to interviews carried out by London Weekend Television's *London Programme* broadcast in February 1991.

Multistorey car parks

Multistorey car parks, a main source of women's fears of using town centres at night, are now acknowledged to be in need of new thinking. In our town reports we recommended that all

towns single out one multistorey for improvement and the provision of additional safety features, and that this car park be
regarded as the 'evening' car park for the town. Among suggestions were better lighting, able-bodied staff (if this seems to go
against the grain of equal-opportunities thinking it is because we
did not feel that the employment of elderly people with dis-
abilities was the most suitable way of encouraging confidence in
the security of car parks), and women-only bays at ground-floor
level next to the staffed exit. This has already been achieved as a
matter of course in some European countries. It is now part of
regional regulations in Dortmund in Germany, for example, to
have women-only bays in all new car parks.

Designing for secure travel

Safe transport, by foot, bicycle, car, taxi, bus or train, always
involves the physical environment surrounding the means of
transport. Atkins (1989) tackled many of these environmental
considerations with insight and panache, and we were very
pleased to be able to echo the findings there, particularly to do
with the design of pedestrian routes, bus and rail termini, and
street lighting, in our own studies.

Lighting

Better lighting always came high on the list of women's priorities for making town centres feel safer and themselves more
secure. The importance of lighting prompted us to organize a
seminar for the participating towns on just this issue; this was led
by Roy Fleming of the Centre for Criminology at Middlesex
Polytechnic, who is one of the main advocates of the use of
lighting strategies to improve urban safety and security. Although the evidence from North America, where most lighting
research has been done, remains inconclusive, it certainly is clear
that improved lighting decreases people's fear of crime, and since
perceptions largely determined people's attitudes towards town-
centre usage, we felt this supported our case for security through
activity and numbers. And although in some experiments better

lighting has been claimed to reduce (or, critics would argue, displace) night-time crime by up to 50 per cent, Fleming's (1987) argument is that what we do know for certain is

in most major towns and cities in Europe that 42% . . . of all night-time street crime takes place when lighting levels are at 5 Lux or below and a further 32% of night-time crime is committed between lighting levels of 5 Lux and 10 Lux, whereas only 3% of these crimes take place where the level of lighting is about 20 Lux.

It would be foolish on this evidence to discount lighting factors in strategies for night-time urban revitalization.

In addition, Fleming argues the cost–benefit case for investment in better public lighting (though, in our experience, such sophisticated urban economics went out of the window years ago in public spending, with the abolition of the metropolitan county councils, competitive tendering, deregulation, rate-capping and privatization programmes reducing everything to 'bottom-line' simplistics). Yet the cost–benefit arguments are wholly persuasive. The cost of lighting a mile of motorway (or, preferably, of pedestrian precinct) is about the same as the cost of running a domestic cooker. The cost of keeping an assault victim in hospital is probably in the region of £300 a week, whereas the cost of one well-placed town-centre floodlight would be less than 20p a week. Fleming's advocacy is based on a strong sense that unless we try using lighting to reduce fear, the spiral of decline in the night-time use of towns and cities will only worsen. It seems to us a compelling case.

Children

Central to all questions of the use of town and city centres by women were questions of childcare and other forms of provision for children. Few shopping centres offered any kind of play areas or facilities, let alone crèches where parents could leave children while they went shopping. Few even had toilets, let alone toilets with nappy-changing facilities. On these and many other issues, people would often exclaim: 'Why do the British hate children so much?' In Stirling a woman interviewed said that the general attitude in both shops and public facilities is that 'children are your responsibility, not ours'. Another Stirling woman summed it up by saying: 'Children are non-persons: they don't spend and they don't vote.' These comments arose with regard to lack of daycare, lack of play facilities, lack of facilities for people pushing prams or buggies, lack of children's menus in restaurants, and in general a dismissive attitude towards children in public places. It was rare to see adults with children *en famille* in the city centre after 6 p.m. when the shops closed.

We were glad to notice small portents of change. The Metro Centre in Gateshead has a shoppers' crèche where children can be left for up to three hours at a reasonably cheap hourly rate. The Centre manager saw this as a crucial element in the success of the store. The Swedish furniture store, IKEA, although currently only having two superstores in Britain, has made the provision of crèche facilities a marketing feature. Mothercare, not surprisingly, runs crèches in some of its stores. However, in none of the other towns we studied did any of the shopping centres provide childcare facilities at the time of the report, though in Basingstoke the Prudential has agreed to run a shoppers' crèche as part of the town-centre improvement campaign. It now seems more likely that crèche facilities will be provided to support parents in their role as consumers, rather than in support of the idea of welfare for children in their own right, as part of the collective responsibility of a society which assumes both parents to be working.

On the other hand, Greenwich Council provided a Christmas shoppers' crèche for Woolwich town-centre users in its Waterfront Leisure Centre, as it does for regular Leisure Centre users, including Monday and Wednesday evenings which are allocated to women-only provision. Here the public sector has taken the lead, with a 1990 sports facility survey showing that 51 per cent of public sector centres had crèche facilities compared to only 29 per cent of private centres.

With the growing number of empty shopfronts which were appearing at the end of 1990 as the recession deepened, it did seem to us a timely opportunity to encourage the use of empty shops for crèches, perhaps run as start-up businesses by locally trained staff. The notion that providing facilities for children is somehow a luxury 'add-on' or extravagance was dispelled for us by the example of the Mosaic Studios in Middlesbrough, a private sector initiative comprising fitness rooms, beauty salons, dance studios, dance classes, hairdressing salons, but built around the provision of all-day childcare available to users and non-users alike at reasonable rates. The owner said she believed that the provision of childcare facilities, well used by local women, had been a key to the success of the overall facility.

In order to give both parents and children a better sense of what was on offer in town centres, we proposed a number of specific recommendations to local authorities, including commissioning a local 'I Spy' book of town-centre buildings, features and facilities, as well as a 'Guide to Children's Facilities', giving details of childcare provision, day nurseries, children's clothes shops and toy shops, a guide to cafés and restaurants that welcomed children and provided children's portions, as well as details of local sports and leisure facilities with programmes aimed at young people.

Women in cities: the double bind

Overwhelmed by the statistical evidence showing the scale of fear among women of going out at night in Britain, and from the several hundred interviews we conducted with women in the 12 towns and cities, we realized that the perspective of women on urban life was quite fundamentally different from that of men, and will have to be addressed as such. For in many ways women are the majority users of town centres for shopping, voluntary activities, and social meetings – but only in the daytime. At night the pubs open, and the town centre once again becomes primarily the domain of men. At night women have to have a reason for being in the town centre; men do not. Part of this inequality arises from the way in which a woman's spending power is often defined as being 'for the family' rather than for herself. In a similar vein, there is still a tendency to associate the 'public' sphere with the world of men, and the 'private' and domestic sphere as solely the preserve and proper place for women.

Towns and cities will not come alive again until they are available to all people to use them freely and without harassment or fear. This recognition clearly now informs much Home Office and other criminological thinking, but we were aware that our approach to revitalization had a different starting point and main premise. For whereas we often came across a concern for urban crime, it seemed based on the idea that high security was a precondition for urban revitalization. We took the opposite point of view, and in one report stated quite crudely that it would not make any difference if there were armed police on the streets of several of our towns – women would still not come into town at night simply because there was nothing worth going into town for. In our view, until there is a genuine choice of activities, entertainment and places where women can meet in towns and cities at night, and provision for children where necessary, then security policies alone will have little if any effect. The 'law and order' paradigm for urban renewal is out-dated; only a people-centred cultural strategy can bring towns and cities back to life.

4

Licensed space

I don't drink, so there's nothing in town for me to do at night.
Middle-aged woman, Middlesbrough (1990)

I told myself too that if I had a young son or daughter whose work took him
or her away from home, to live in one of these towns, I should object if it
were a Sabbatarian town of this kind, which could offer its young folk
nothing on Sunday night but a choice between monkey-parading and du-
bious pubs. Please give me, I would say, a wicked wide-open city, busy
dishonouring its Sabbath, blazing with lights on Sunday evening, with
concerts, theatre, cinemas, dance halls, restaurants, in full naughty swing.
There I could trust my innocent child. But not – oh, never – in this barbaric
gloom and boredom.
J.B. Priestley, English Journey (1934)

One of the key reasons given by a number of local authorities for participating in the *Out of Hours* project was that it might offer them strategies for coping with the problem of town centres being increasingly dominated by youth drinking, noisy pubs, nightclubs, and occasional violence. The so-called 'lager lout' phenomenon of the 1980s, whether real or imagined, was certainly seen as an issue in Preston, Middlesbrough, Liverpool, Swansea, Reading, Basingstoke, Southend, Luton and Gloucester – significantly all free-standing and self-contained towns and cities – where local newspapers were often full of stories of youth gangs, street-fighting, hostility towards the police, drunkenness and violence.

The sense that town-centre evening life has been hijacked or colonized by the young at the expense of all other sections of the population has come across strongly in many of the interviews. Older people talked of no longer wishing to go into town to visit the cinema or theatre or to eat out because of the potential fear of being accosted by gangs of young people (or having their cars broken into); many people do find groups of young men jostling and shouting in the streets frightening, added to which public swearing is to many almost as upsetting as physical aggression. In Preston a couple attending a Masonic Lodge dance talked about taking a taxi from the multistorey car park to a club 200 yards away rather than walking through the town centre; in Swansea pedestrians and even motorists will always take the long way round the Kingsway at night. The numbers of young people involved are astonishing: in Middlesbrough and Preston these run to several thousands on Thursday, Friday and Saturday night, and in Swansea we were told that it could reach 5000. What for young people is now an exuberant form of weekend behaviour – having a good time, creating a carnival atmosphere on the streets every week – is perceived by others as territorial colonization underscored by the threat of violence. Who swears wins.

Local fears have been compounded by national publicity. In 1987 the Association of Chief Police Officers (ACPO) commissioned a study of the subject, and in June of that year reported that

A special police survey reveals an alarming picture of nationwide disorder in once-tranquil small towns and rural areas in England and Wales . . . No longer is spontaneous disorder confined to inner cities and large towns. Groups of usually young and often drunk people gather to fight each other, and to attack police and property in a way that was a rarity even as recently as ten years ago.

As a result the Home Office commissioned a more detailed study, *Drinking and Disorder: A Study of Non-metropolitan Violence*

(Tuck 1989). The towns in the *Out of Hours* study mostly fit the criteria for 'non-metropolitan' used in these studies.

Drinking and Disorder

One of the main findings of the Home Office report was that although heavy drinking was a year-round phenomenon in the towns studied (all in the South of England), incidents of disorder were mostly seasonal: 42 per cent of the incidents requiring police action happened between May and August. Not surprisingly, most took place either on a Friday or Saturday night, a finding recently confirmed in Conflict and Violence in Pubs, MCM Research 1990, which reported that 45 per cent of violent incidents happened between 10 and 11 p.m. on Fridays and Saturdays. The study concentrated almost exclusively on behaviour in and around pubs rather than nightclubs; the two seem to have very different patterns of behaviour associated with them, though in Middlesbrough and Swansea the line between what is a pub and what is a club seems blurred. Certainly nightclubs are much more likely to be under local ownership – we talked to local club owners in Liverpool, Preston, Stirling and Southend, and know from other sources that the clubs in Middlesbrough and Swansea are nearly all owned by local entrepreneurs.

Local owners have more invested – not just financially – in maintaining a good local reputation, whereas pub managers seem to change with great frequency. In the MCM research a correlation was found between high turnover of managers and high levels of violence. In Swansea a long-standing suburban publican told us that years ago he knew every town-centre pub manager personally – they would meet regularly in each other's pubs – and now he knew none. Yet 'bad management' of pubs was an important factor in the situation that might lead to trouble and disorder, according to the Home Office report (Tuck 1989). Many managers we spoke to regard the 'happy hour' promotions of some town centre pubs as irresponsible (not a wholly disinterested response!) since they encouraged early evening drinking of large quantities of spirits – doubles or even trebles for the price of a single measure.

Other local surveys of these issues – The Working Party on Disorder in Hull City Centre (1990), the Newport Alcohol Abuse & Social Disorder Demonstration Project (1990) – have highlighted the potentially dangerous role of poorly trained and casually recruited security staff or 'bouncers'. In some Hull pubs the research team found it impossible to identify security staff at all by dress, and this, they felt, contributed to potential violence, as customers resented being stopped from going in by people they initially thought were simply other customers. In Manchester the problems associated with violence on the club scene, often involving a dangerous mixture of drugs, guns and dubious bouncers, has caused several clubs to close voluntarily.

Which young people?

Drinking and Disorder (Tuck 1989) identified different groups (called 'circuit groups') of young people in the towns they studied: first, the all-male, loud-swearing and often tattooed groups who caused most of the trouble; second the 'top man' group, better dressed and less violent; third the 'posers' in mixed-sex groups with expensive fashionable clothes; and fourth, miscellaneous groups of punks, students and eccentrics, who were mostly little trouble at all. It is clear from this report that only a minority of young people 'on the town' at night are potentially violent or troublesome – and, in fact, these can often be identified in advance. The Newport study (1990) rightly points out that an arrest or caution rate of not more than 20 young people out of some 4,000 drinking in town each weekend attests to the fact that the very great majority cause no problems at all.

The Home Office report (Tuck 1989) noted the pattern for town-centre pubs to be converted into 'youth-pubs' or 'disco-pubs' and thought that 'this kind of movement of the market is probably irresistible'. They cited the case of the town-centre pub manager who converted his quiet pub into a 'disco-pub' and was able to make enough money in his first year to buy a bar in Spain. In Middlesbrough, we were told, 'what starts as a wine bar always ends up as a disco'. But here again we confront the dilemma that market forces and short-term developments, left to run unchecked, can cause long-term damage to wider public and social interests. We must remember also, as the report points out, that this 'pattern of entertainment drinking seems peculiar to the United Kingdom. In Europe there is no regular closing time; so one does not get the sudden exodus on to the streets.'

Drinking time

Much of the trouble connected with youth drinking is, then, related to closing time. Pub opening hours are once again a subject for debate following the relaxation of licensing hours in August 1988, when pubs in England and Wales were allowed to stay open 'all day' from 11 a.m. to 11 p.m. This legislation was brought in earlier in Scotland. As yet the effects of all-day opening are a matter of speculation rather than actual study, although in our research we found patterns of town–centre usage already affected by these changes. The origin of strict opening and closing times in Britain (compared with many other countries) is partly a response to the teetotal movement which swept Britain in the nineteenth century and partly a measure by the Lloyd George government during the First World War to stop people drinking so much. 'We are fighting Germany, Austria and drink, and the greatest of these deadly foes is drink,' he said.

Opening times are not just a matter of convenience. They reflect a peculiarly ambivalent attitude to drink, also strongly represented in the architectural styles of British pubs. The teetotal movement convinced many that drink was inherently evil rather than a problem only of excess, and the strict regulation of times and places exemplifies this. People are not trusted to choose their own times of leisure; drink licences are granted only under the most arcane of legislative powers which strongly differentiate drinking from a fatal combination with entertainment, singing or dancing. It is still illegal to sing in most pubs.

All-day opening

All-day opening has helped relax attitudes slightly, although the increased reliance of pub turnover on food has probably had a greater effect on pub life. In our study we noted that in some towns afternoon drinking had created a new kind of urban timetable for some people, particularly the unemployed, whereby they would come into the town centre late in the morning, sign on if necessary, do their shopping and then meet friends for a drink and a chat in the early afternoon. In one or two pubs it was evident that the 'high point' of the day was about 4 p.m., when the pub was busiest, before people left to go home for tea and probably spend the rest of the evening watching television or listening to music at home.

Pub architecture

The design and architecture of British pubs has evolved over time, producing a wide variety of external appearances and histories, but inside a number of now fairly standard formats. The traditional town pub, at one time consisting of as many as six or seven quite distinct 'spaces' or territories, each with its own rules and codes of behaviour – public, tap, saloon, snug, games room, women's room, jug and bottle, lounge, club room or masonic room – has in recent years in many pubs been opened out into one large general area. Ostensibly creating a more open and public realm, the result has often been that one kind of user or crowd can quickly predominate and establish the codes of behaviour for everybody else. In the older segmented pub there were opportunities for people to be noisy or quiet as they wished, to play cards or darts, for women to meet, for business to be done, all in the same pub but separately. The open-plan pub denies these opportunities. This is a major loss to mixed usage, and perhaps one of the greatest contributory factors to many people feeling that 'the young' have taken over, as indeed they have done in many town-centre pubs.

The opaque glass and curtained windows and doors which are a feature of nearly all British pubs (again in contrast to European bars), sharply separates the inside of the pub from the street outside; in reality the pub turns its back on the street. There are rarely chairs and tables outside pubs. When a stranger enters a pub he or she is entering unknown territory, and often has no indication at all from outside as to what kind of atmosphere or clientele is to be found within. It is not surprising that most women would not dare go into a strange pub alone.

A number of women we talked to about pubs strongly resented this feeling of deliberate exclusion. One woman journalist living in Woolwich spoke about how, on very hot summer days, many town-centre pubs propped their doors open, but all that could be seen from outside was a dark space where men seemed to be drinking in a very private club-like ambience. She felt completely excluded. Others talked about the resentment among women struggling with children and shopping past pubs full of men and noisy laughter which only exacerbated their feeling of exclusion from social life. Yet in Middlesbrough a new pub which opened with a conservatory-style glass frontage was quickly taken over by groups of women who clearly felt safer having a drink but in full view of the street outside. One large pub in Woolwich, which also has a conservatory extension at the back, was mentioned by several women as the only pub they would enter alone.

It is vital to think more seriously about the reaction of young women to the 'lager culture' where it exists. What did they really think about the atmosphere and ambience of the crowded, noisy pubs? Some initial impressions from Preston and Liverpool suggest that often young women are disappointed and embarrassed by their male peers' excessive drinking. But what alternatives for young women currently exist? The success of wine bars in many towns is partly to do with a new kind of architectural style. Most wine bars cultivate an open style that allows the passer-by to see inside and make a decision to enter with some degree of confidence. Potted plants, food, framed pictures, tablecloths all create a less threatening and more domestic ambience. Tea and coffee are also more readily available in wine bars. It is not surprising that women prefer them. In some towns women told us that they felt safe in certain theatre bars such as the Grand in Swansea, the Royal Exchange theatre in Manchester, the Everyman Bistro in Liverpool, and more generally in hotel lobbies and bars rather than pubs and clubs.

Few pubs have children's rooms. The British pub, unlike its European counterpart, is no place for the family. The puritan tradition prefers, it seems, that men drink apart from their families, assuming that young people would be compromised by seeing people drinking, rather than considering that male drinking might be moderated by being a part of a more mixed family and community setting. Yet there are increasingly settings – restaurants, steak-houses, pizza parlours, leisure-centre restaurants – where families can eat and drink together, and these would seem to be preferable in terms of getting away from the male youth drinking phenomenon. The Harvester chain of pub restaurants is growing rapidly by appealing to a family market.

Changing names

But pubs have a symbolic importance far beyond their functional role in providing drink and food. They are often among the oldest buildings in town centres and are therefore regarded as local landmarks. Most people in each town will have used some town-centre pubs at some time in their lives – as youngsters, for a birthday celebration, a wedding – and will have memories associated with them. Stop and ask people for directions in town and you will often be directed along a succession of pub names: 'Go past the George until you get to the traffic lights, then turn left along by the Ship Aground, and walk down there until you get to the Albion. The place you want is next door.'

Many of these names are now changing, and this has caused considerable confusion and even bitterness among older people. Pubs which for 200 years were called the Cricketers are now Sabrina's; the Red Lion overnight became Fat Harry's. As the brewers have honed in on the youth market, so pubs have been refashioned in a completely new image and themed along American or cocktail bar styles. No doubt in the future these stylings will be changed again, but the loss of such an important set of public reference points – and lexicography – has in some cases been traumatic. People cannot keep up with the pace of changing names and identities: it is no longer just the shops which change names every other year, but the pubs as well.

The pub repertoire

The activities which town-centre pubs encourage can have a considerable effect on the likelihood of violent or anti-social behaviour. Several reports have noted that pool tables are often a primary source of conflict, especially where there is no managed order of booking or where bets are surreptitiously laid. On the other hand, in nearly every town studied the pub quiz network has become very strong, and this has given another function to pub life which is certainly undisruptive as well as profitable.

In most towns studied there was at least one pub which regularly featured live music, mostly local bands playing to keen groups of local followers. These pubs often had a slightly down-at-heel image, and the police sometimes assumed and acted upon the assumption that some soft drug dealing was going on, but they were rarely sites of serious trouble, and were often located well away from the 'circuit' pubs. Given the considerable amount of self-organization involved in running a live music venue – booking bands, setting up PA systems, advertising in the press, making touring arrangements – nearly always done by young people themselves at personal expense, it was surprising how little effort had been made by local authorities, youth service, police, and so on, to support and encourage these networks. Yet they were among the most stable youth networks we encountered.

During the course of the study the karaoke craze began to catch on – pubs featuring backing tapes to which users could sing their favourite songs – and again this seemed to add that element of entertainment that marked the difference between having a good night out and simply going drinking. Adding entertainment to the repertoire of pub life is perhaps the best antidote to violence. This is the assumption made by three Hull promoters – Paul Jackson, proprietor of the New Adelphi Club; Tim Maitland, Viking FM Sports Editor; and Charles Waterhouse, local DJ – who reported on youth drinking to the Council's Working Party on City Centre Disorder (Jackson et al. 1990). Their case study was the Hull University Union bar, where, before a wide programme of events was introduced, incidents of trouble, disorder, drunkenness and violence were much more common. The worst incidents were always related to brewery-sponsored drink promotions where students were encouraged to drink as much as possible by specially reduced prices. These promotions have now been banned and free live entertainment and quizzes introduced. Levels of disorder have been greatly reduced, with no noticeable downturn in bar takings. The report concludes that the provision of entertainment is the most effective way of countering disorder resulting from drinking.

Pubs have also found a new role in some towns as theatre and live cabaret venues. The growth of 'alternative comedy' in the 1980s has revived old performance skills and the audience for stand-up comedy and music, and again pubs where these acts featured regularly were not usually associated with trouble. The main problem is that so much depends on having an adventurous manager or licensee who is prepared to work at creating a different kind of venue rather than putting in a sound system, promoting strong lager, putting bouncers on the door and leaving it at that. The large brewery companies continue, understandably, to resist the break-up of their monopoly position as both providers of drink and controllers of the outlets; in the long run, though, diversity of venues in towns will depend on local initiative rather than on corporate plans developed remotely at company headquarters. The stranglehold which pubs have on British evening life must be challenged.

Public transport and locational issues

The Home Office report suggested, among other things, two particular strategies for avoiding conflict and violence in the short term. The first was the need to have 'a sufficiency of public transport away from the entertainment centre late at night if disorder is to be prevented'. The second concerns planning and public space issues. The Home Office noted in the towns it studied that there were certain natural 'cluster points' where people gathered in the daytime and evening to wait, meet and gossip, but there were also obvious 'congestion points' where crowds or groups coming from different directions might collide, become squeezed, interrupt each other's flow, and that where the two different spaces coincided, trouble was likely to occur. 'Location', they argued, 'is clearly crucial to the incidence of disorder.'

The report went on to suggest how planners should avoid accidentally creating 'congestion points', and they also argue strongly that 'Too often the need for such spaces [cluster points] is forgotten in modern town planning, which is built around daytime not evening or entertainment use. Town and village planners need to recover the art of planning for natural social gatherings.' It is gratifying to realize that our preoccupation with the forms and meanings of public space has been ratified by a specific study such as this. Space and time, the two key co-ordinates in this study, again provide the key to the resolution of so many of the current problems.

In Newport the multi-agency team looking into the problem of town-centre drinking suggested a pilot project involving lay-ing on extra public transport at closing time. The bus companies would only agree to the experiment (and contribute financially) if the pubs and clubs as the main beneficiaries of youth drinking, also made a financial contribution. Only two licensees were prepared to pay even the smallest amount – £10 an evening – so the project came to nothing. Yet it should be borne in mind as a strategy in future policies.

Police attitudes

Police attitudes seemed to be fairly similar in the different towns: 'There's a lot of them, but there's not much trouble, and it's only young people having a good time. What's new?' Yet when pressed, deeper reservations emerge. In Swansea we were told that although the police keep a low profile – vans and cars parked in side-streets in case of trouble – there is an underlying fear that one evening an incident will get out of hand and 'the whole thing will blow up'. The whole thing in Swansea in-volves 5000 young people who have been drinking for most of the night. This apprehension is voiced in the Home Office study, which said that 'the case studies recorded in this report suggest the potential for such incidents is regularly there every Friday or Saturday in many – if not most – of the many entertainment centres, some large, some small, in non-metropolitan England and Wales.'

In Middlesbrough what worried the police was that by taking a 'softly, softly' approach, policing by consent and negotiation rather than by force, they were frequently condoning actual criminal offences, mainly indecency (urinating in the streets) and under-age drinking (to start asking everybody in a crowded pub for proof of age could be to invite trouble). And in turn they were accused of dereliction of duty by shopkeepers who in the mornings often found their shop doorways awash with vomit and urine, occasionally windows broken, the streets and pavements littered with cans and chip wrappers, and the general appearance of a town centre after a hurricane. So for the police there is a real problem.

The excellent Hull study recommended better street lighting and the provision of *pissoir*-type urinals in pub districts as a way of encouraging young people not to urinate in the street, for often the young drinkers could genuinely claim that there was nowhere else to go – all the public toilets being closed at night.

One drink problem which has produced very strong policing measures has been daytime drinking in the streets by young people, who may, when drunk, cause offence to passers-by or create a threatening or intimidating presence in town centres. The issue was first brought to national attention by Coventry City Council when, after two years of campaigning, it persuaded the Home Office in early 1988 to conduct an experiment in banning the drinking of alcohol in public in the city centre, an experiment now being followed in six other town centres. People found drinking are cautioned by a police officer and, if they persist, arrested and subsequently fined. Similar laws obtain in most cities in the United States. The scheme seems punitive, particularly since it could appear to result from a failure by all authorities to plan for worthwhile alternatives to long-term youth unemployment, often the main factor in producing the groups of young people hanging around town centres during the day. In Woolwich one of the police officers we spoke to admitted that at times there was a problem of drunks in the main

General Gordon Square during the daytime, and sometimes they moved them on, but he also noted that when the square was being well used by other people in the summer, having picnic lunches, sunbathing, sitting out, the drunks moved elsewhere of their own accord. These are deeply territorial issues, underestimated by planners, but the reclamation of town space has to be less a question of prohibitive legislation and more one of creating a felt sense of ownership and belonging.

The economics and demographics of drinking in Britain

Drinking in Britain is big business. According to a Mintel Report, *The On Trade Revolution* (1988), more than £13 billion passed over the counters of pubs and other licensed premises in 1987. This is not surprising when one looks at people's leisure preferences as detailed by Central Statistical Office (1989) – in every single age group, except among women over 60, 'going out for a drink' was the most reported activity in out-of-home leisure behaviour. Among males aged 20–29, 87 per cent had been to a pub in the four weeks before being interviewed (other activities were cinema, 16 per cent; theatre/opera/ballet, 5 per cent; dancing, 13 per cent; and going out for a meal, 56 per cent). And in the same report detailing household expenditure on selected leisure items, spending on alcohol consumed away from home was the largest item of expenditure when averaged out over all households. So not only do pubs predominate socially in evening life and culture, they also dominate leisure economically.

Yet beneath the monolithic pattern of drink-dominated leisure, new trends are stirring. The Mintel Report cited above argued that 'if the profitability of the industry is to be sustained, the historic male-dominated pub-culture forbidding to women and families must change'. For the threat to the traditional pub market is increasingly coming from more activity-based venues which also offer places for drinking – sports centres, leisure centres, theatres and music venues. According to a report from Projection 2000 (1990), *Leisure Centres*, the leisure centre is set to oust the pub as the UK's traditional social meeting place by the year 2000. Interestingly, the single European market of 1992, according to experts, is not going to lead to a rush of *Red Lions* or *Dog and Trumpets* in Siena or Darmstadt, rather the trend will be the reverse: European firms with real expertise in bars/cafés, wine bars and family restaurants will make the running in the UK, or, to put it in the jargon of the marketing manager of Boddingtons Breweries: 'If anything the impact of foreign travel has been to Europeanize the drinking experience in the UK.' The new 'state-of-the-art pub', according to Whitbread, will be a community pub aimed at attracting women, families and irregular pub visitors, with 'coffee, croissants and flowery wallpaper'.

Whether significant historical differences with regard to pubs between the North and South of England will continue to buck these national trends remains to be seen. But statistical evidence with regard to changing patterns of youth drinking also anticipates continued decline. According to an article in *Marketing Week* by planning consultant John Howkins in April 1990, the moral panic about rising youth drunkenness is a myth. Howkins states that 'Convictions for drunkenness offences have declined by 25% since their peak in the early Eighties, and the amount of alcohol consumed by the younger generation (defined here as 18–24-year-olds) has declined dramatically in the past ten years.' The average consumption of young people has fallen from 17.2 units of alcohol per week in 1978 to 14.3 units per week in 1987. The Henley Centre for Social Forecasting has predicted that while the 15–24 old age group was responsible for 32 per cent of total pub visits in 1989, this will decline to 27.5 per cent of total pub visits by 1995. If these trends are taken with other demographic changes under way in the British population, then the current phenomenon of youth drinking and town-centre domination may well have peaked. This means that alternative scenarios for town-centre evening life once again become a real possibility.

5

The invisible web

Voluntary work is an important part of people's social life nowadays. They don't go to the pub or the cinema, they go to meetings.

Volunteer Organizer, Swansea (1990)

A starting point is Burke's 'little platoons', the germ of wider public affections. It is in small groups where people learn participation, leadership, collective aims and goals. In this perspective, a flourishing political community will be a mosaic of smaller collectivities, which act as nurseries for the feelings of mutual loyalty and trust which hold the wider community together, and where the skills of self-government may be learned and practised.

David Marquand, The Unprincipled Society *(1988)*

The voluntary and self-organized tradition

The principles of self-organization and of independence from the state are claimed as legitimate traditions by both Right and Left in British politics. The Right has proclaimed the virtues of self-help while the Left has celebrated the efficiency and social values of mutual aid. The amateur tradition in sports, the voluntary tradition in social welfare, the participatory and amateur tradition in the arts and crafts, have all contributed to the high level of involvement by people in making and remaking their own social life of leisure, entertainment and social welfare. The roots of this still enlivening principle of local life are variously to

be found in the Protestant tradition of good works, the noncon-
formist tradition of independent institutions, the radical ethic of
Chartist and trade union self-organization and the Victorian
principle of self-help. It is a heady mixture.

In all of the towns and cities studied, the voluntary sector
appeared strong and thriving, though there were major differences in attitude towards the voluntary sector by the local authority in each town, not necessarily on the basis of party politics.
This was something that emerged on many occasions – the
degree to which the political complexion of the local council
was not a sure indicator or benchmark of the ideology of the
actual policies pursued. Some Conservative councils were highly
interventionist, while some Labour councils appeared *laissez-
faire*, while with regard to support for the voluntary sector each
town had to be examined on its own terms. It would be fair to
say, however, that there was often a degree of tension.

Local government, on the defensive for so long now, sometimes perceived the voluntary sector as a rebellious army in
waiting, ready to take oer any of the functions of local government that national government might wish to determine. In
other ways voluntary organizations were perceived as 'vocif-
erous minorities' or 'troublemakers', attempting to interfere in
the policies and programmes of a local authority democratically
elected and responsible to the wider electorate. Only slowly
were local authorities learning that they themselves had to work
in partnership with other bodies: that the era of the powerful
municipal government setting the whole of the local civic and
cultural agenda had come to an end. It was still possible to ask
senior local authority officers or local politicians about arts and
cultural provision in a town and to find that they automatically
defined it as what the council provided, no more, no less. This
attitude is no longer helpful.

The logic of this kind of thinking often meant that local
listings guides or 'What's On' monthly bulletins distributed free
by local authorities only listed events and facilities they provided, omitting to mention the many more activities offered by
the voluntary, independent or commercial sectors. The result
was that one might only find two performances, concerts, shows
or activities listed for an evening in a town with a population of

150,000 when in reality there might be twenty or thirty. The assumption that the interests and priorities of the local authority and of the local population always coincided continued to create problems. It also produced resentments, particularly by younger people who saw their cultural interests – live music, dance clubs, record-dealing, cabaret, fashion – at best ignored, at worst derided by those involved in local government.

Participation: the national picture

For many people participation in voluntary organizations takes up a significant part of their free time. Decline in membership among some kinds of organization such as the Mothers' Union, Women's Institute, and Townswomen's Guild, has been matched by increases in others such as the Civic Trust (250,000 members), the National Trust (1.5 million members), the Ramblers' Association (57,000 members) and the Royal Society for the Protection of Birds (561,000 members). Involvement in outdoor and environmental organizations has increased dramatically in the past decade. Self-help and voluntary welfare organizations such as Al-Anon family groups (952 branches), Relate (166 branches), Cruse (73 branches) and the Samaritans (182 branches), have also seen large increases in membership. The National Federation of Music Societies has over 1200 affiliated groups representing amateur choirs and orchestras throughout the country; it has been estimated that there are some 17,000 amateur operatic and dramatic societies involving nearly 3 million people annually in amateur performance.

Participation: a Southend case study

In all of the towns and cities a questionnaire was circulated to a wide range of local voluntary organizations, asking for details concerning the age of the organization, current membership and problems encountered in sustaining activities, as well as for personal responses to a list of questions about use of the town centre at night. The survey in Southend was typical. Of 150 questionnaires distributed (by no means the total number of voluntary organizations in the town), some 60 were returned, a high rate of return for this kind of survey.

Most organizations had been established over 25 years, and each succeeding decade produced slightly fewer new organizations to the extent that only three claimed to have been formed in the five years prior to the survey. This pyramid shape was to be expected, but the very low number of new organizations responding was worrying. Such new organizations as there were seemed to represent campaigning groups around the 'new agenda' of social issues – women's aid, disabled rights and other self-help groups. New arts or cultural organizations seemed rare, or were perhaps resistant to providing information about themselves.

From figures given for membership – active, occasional and mailing list numbers – several thousand Southend people appeared to be involved in voluntary organizations: we estimated between 3000 and 8000, in a town with a population of 165,000 in total. Many clubs, societies, charities and self-help groups obviously had overlapping memberships, but a strong impression was given of a large invisible web of activity covering all aspects of amateur arts, leisure and social welfare that provided the town with a civil society of its own. Organizations responding included a number of amateur drama and opera groups, religious organizations, self-help welfare organizations, sports clubs, hobby groups and local charities.

Among the problems which many organizations faced, 'difficulties in recruiting new members' was raised by a number of them (although it seemed to be in the nature of the voluntary sector to be in permanent organizational and membership crisis), exacerbated, many felt, by genuine difficulties with regard to the decline of public transport and fears for safety about on the streets at night. Indeed, from the survey it was clear that this was an almost exclusively car-owning and car-using sector, and those without access to cars were no longer active in voluntary organizations.

Organizations recruited overwhelmingly by 'word of mouth', and the degree to which voluntary life was rooted in – and possibly in itself sustained – the social lives of most respondents and members came across strongly. This was particularly evident when it came to fundraising; it transpired that while the majority of organizations were financially self-sustaining, not only was fundraising a major part of the social calendar, but in some cases possibly the main *raison d'être*. It was organizational life itself rather than the espoused cause or interest which often seemed to provide the main focus for people's commitment and involvement.

When asked as individuals what their main form of social activity was, the majority claimed that it was connected with attending socials, functions and meetings of voluntary organizations, significantly ahead of visits to the cinema, theatre and other activities. This degree of participation in voluntary organizations as a main form of social life also came across in replies to a question which asked respondents to list, in order of most frequent participation over the previous three months, seven different kinds of activity: 'attending voluntary clubs, organizations and societies' came well ahead of 'watching TV/video/ listening to radio at home' or 'cinema/theatre/live concerts' and 'eating out/going to pub/meeting friends somewhere' and other choices.

Admittedly the sample was small, self-selecting to a large degree, and certainly very active in local life; nevertheless, the importance which people attached to voluntary activity was surprising, and the degree to which it flourished almost entirely outside the local political realm and without any kind of strategic support from local government salutary. It could be argued that what seemed to be flourishing without support should be best left alone, but there were other factors which demonstrated that support and occasionally intervention could be beneficial to the sector, particularly in dealing with issues of public safety, provision of meeting places, and even occasionally professional animation to get things going. Going out at night was seen as a major issue and a real disincentive to voluntary activity; transport and availability of meeting rooms were frequently mentioned as urgent problems; lack of information and inappropriate forms of advertising and local information services were seen as obstacles to increasing membership. And the strength of the amateur musical world in Southend was partly attributable to local government encouragement in the form of having the only professional music director on the staff of a local authority in Britain.

The existence of this unique post is proof, indeed, that traditions can be invented. Southend is nationally renowned for the strength and high quality of its many amateur choirs, orchestras and music clubs. The Southend Boys' Choir is internationally known. The Southend Music Club has over 2000 members, and large-scale choral performances are regularly held in the town. Lunchtime concerts and recitals are held in the town hall for town-hall workers. Amateur opera is on the programme frequently at the Cliffs Pavilion and the Westcliff Palace Theatre. Yet this long-standing 'tradition' is perhaps only 25 years old and derives from the pioneering enthusiasm of a small number of music professionals with support from the Council to build the amateur music scene in Southend and to give it a national reputation.

It is true that the Southend rock music scene (itself also nationally renowned in the 1960s) has been ignored or cold-shouldered in the main programme of activities and financial support, and that is a criticism which still stands, but with regard to the classical tradition, Southend is an extraordinary example of how thriving 'amateur' arts cultures can be encouraged into being and supported from then on.

Amateur and professional arts

Involvement in the arts is a key social and leisure activity in people's free time, whether as participants or as observers, even though the very word 'arts' creates problems of definition and association which continue to exercise the minds of practitioners, funding bodies and policy-makers alike. For the purposes of our study, we favoured a very wide definition that included all creative activities from knitting, home photography and brass band music to video production, four-track sound recording, avant-garde theatre and professional opera. All these things matter to their participants and followers in equal ways, and all play an important part in the cultural life of the town or city.

85

Yet arts policy, at local and national levels, has been be-devilled by the divide between amateur and professional arts. The origins of the Arts Council are to be found in the Council for the Encouragement of Music and the Arts (CEMA), a war-time organization established to promote the amateur arts dur-ing the war to raise morale. Yet as soon as the Arts Council was established after the war it quickly rid itself of any commitment to amateur performance and rapidly turned its attention to sup-porting the professional arts exclusively. Nearly fifty years later it is only belatedly coming to recognize the important role which amateur participation plays in creating a wider interest in the classical musical repertoire and in the local provision of light opera, musical comedy and mainstream drama, some of which has proved to be of a very high standard indeed, particularly in choral work. Many professional classical recordings rely on ama-teur choirs.

Other problems of classification, such as the self-limiting dis-tinction between arts and crafts (with two separate national or-ganizations) have also exacerbated the division between more intellectual forms of artistic practice, such as sculpture, and more hobby-based work, such as marquetry or embroidery. The latter can be every bit as artistic and imaginative as the former, but their domestic and popular historical roots have caused them to be excluded from the canon of taste or repertoire of accepted cultural forms. A recent Crafts Council touring exhibition de-voted to knitting, 'The Common Stitch', attracted enthusiastic crowds wherever it went, a testament to the interest in this allegedly 'ordinary' craft and domestic skill and to the recog-nition, at long last, of the technical and aesthetic achievements of much 'amateur' work. In Middlesbrough, for example, there was a thriving lace-making network, which received only oc-casional acknowledgement from the public galleries, exhibition spaces, arts administrators or funding agencies. Yet it was a craft and an arena of aesthetic discrimination that had strong local roots.

Most young rock bands were also 'amateur', in the sense that their members had received little musical education or training, were largely self-taught, and played in addition to holding down other jobs or were unemployed. Yet the role they played in local youth cultures was dynamic and important. In Middlesbrough a well-organized local music collective put on concerts, collectively owned a good public address system, and helped bands make demo tapes. To its credit, Middlesbrough Council was increasingly keen to support them. In some towns grants and other forms of support were made to the thriving amateur operatic and dramatic clubs (most towns had between ten and thirty such local groups), whereas in other towns this amateur activity was ignored. Funding for the arts took the form of support for theatres and large halls offering a programme of mainstream professional theatre, comedy and light entertainment.

Libraries, theatres, galleries and museums

All towns and cities had libraries, theatres, art galleries and museums, as part of the traditional civic culture available to local people, and which took the bulk of local spending on 'the arts'. In many places library provision was in fact part of the county council service, and invariably this created real problems of coordination with the towns' own cultural amenities. In a number of towns these facilities were often located close to each other, forming a civic area often along with the town hall, and in some places the rest of the town centre was moving away from them, leaving them isolated from the main centre of activity. In Swansea the library and Glynn Vivian Art Gallery had been left stranded as each wave of new developments took place further away towards the seafront and the Maritime Quarter. Casual use of the gallery was in steep decline, as there were no longer the same numbers of passers-by. The Beecroft Art Gallery in Southend was well away from the town centre and had little casual use.

But everywhere it was clear that the central library remained the key public cultural institution of all, the one place (the last place?) where one would find a genuine cross-section of people by age, class and ethnic origin, and which would have to be a central factor in any programme of urban revitalization. Nationally a third of the population use public libraries on a

87

regular basis, and in some of the towns we surveyed the proportion was higher. No other cultural venue of any kind in Britain – theatre, cinema, bowling alley, concert hall, art gallery, football stadium, bingo hall – attracts anything like this proportion of the population. It seemed ironic, given this success story, that library provision was so under threat from public expenditure cuts involving redundancies, shorter opening hours, fewer book purchases, and closure of services such as reference sections. Where library provision has been extended and modernized, such as in Hounslow's marvellous Centre Space, an even wider cross-section of the population has made the public library a main reason for its use of the town centre apart from shopping. Older men come in regularly to browse through the newspapers, and the younger people meet their friends after school to chat, do homework and date each other. Muslims particularly regarded the library as a respectable place, not associated with drink, and often one of the few town-centre venues they and their children felt free to use.

The public library was not only a key cultural space but also a key public space, where people could meet, browse, read the papers, listen to children's storytelling, study local history, seek reference information, find out what was going on in town, take away a list of voluntary organizations, borrow books, records and even videos, in some places have a snack or a cup of coffee, where women could wait unharassed and pensioners could keep out of the cold. Extending opening hours and services, we concluded, was a priority for giving people back their town centres. The public library should be a flagship for cultural choice and diversity in any revived civic culture, as it was often both the heart and the brain of local public life. In the United States, Partners for Liveable Place, one of the key urban renewal agencies, has joined with the American Public Library Association to campaign for the vital role that libraries play in sustaining viable communities.

Adult education

In describing the typical townscape of the Victorian city, Mark Girouard (1990) recognized the many buildings were put up

to feed the nineteenth-century capacity for intellectual en-
lightenment and endeavour.

The pursuit of knowledge was as important to the Victorians as
the pursuit of health, and the results were obvious in the towns.
It led to buildings of many types, catering for all classes: schools,
colleges, universities, museums, art galleries, and institutes of
various kinds including Mechanics' Institutes.

That architectural legacy was still to be found in most towns.
But the activities these buildings supported were under severe
pressure.

In Manchester, for the first time ever, the city's education
department failed to produce a guide to local evening classes
because of budgetary constraints. Adult education everywhere
was under threat of severe diminution or even closure. Pressure
came not only from the providers but also from related costs
involved in attending classes. In Swansea we were told: 'The
high cost of bus fares is on the agenda of every further and adult
education meeting.'

Yet like the voluntary sector, it had created in many towns a
unique public sphere of evening activity, some of it vocational,
providing opportunities for people to seek the qualifications
needed to enable them to get better jobs, much of it non-
vocational and related to interests – learning foreign languages,
studying local history, cookery classes, literature, photography
– that enabled people to lead more interesting and informed
lives. In Southend we were told that nearly 8000 adults partici-
pated in daytime and evening classes. This was clearly an important choice of free-time activity that regularly brought
people out of their homes and into the public realm. In 1991 it
was announced that more than half a million places on part-
time and evening classes would disappear; in some places –
Hampshire, for example – all adult education may well be
closed down. What this means is fewer people going out in the
evening, and therefore more fear on the streets for those who
still do.

Festivals

What we called the 'invisible web' of voluntary activity was made visible from time to time during local carnivals, festivals and fairs. It was only then that people had an opportunity to realize the extent of this hidden public realm, something we felt should occur more frequently. Not surprisingly, it was the local festival – the Southend Carnival, the Middlesbrough Festival, Woolwich Week – that most people mentioned when asked to name the most important event in the annual civic calendar. Nearly all these annual festivals created opportunities for local clubs and societies, charities and amateur groups, to organize stalls, recruit members and generally advertise their existence. Each festival acted as a kind of mirror which allowed the town's organizations and their members to see themselves as part of a wider community.

Festivals and carnivals were also a rare occasion when public space could be reappropriated by the people: high streets and town centres closed to cars, and used for parades, large gatherings, funfairs, children's events, live concerts and open-air services. Carnivals emphasize, in the words of Jenni Francis (1991), an arts marketing specialist,

---

the social aspect of entertainment . . . best demonstrated in the success of carnivals and loosely structured music events among the Afro-Caribbean community and the parallel success of Bhangra events in the Asian community. The enduring perception of family celebrations as the best opportunities for cultural affirmation continues to sustain the visible minority communities.

This important elision between art, culture and entertainment, exhibited during carnivals and festivals, ought, we felt, to be a greater priority for local arts policy throughout the year, yet often the budget available for festivals and carnivals was a tiny fraction of that available for building-based provision which often reached no more than 1–5 per cent of the local population.

Experiments in open-air provision, and in the use of portable venues, have shown that large audiences, both during the day and at night, can be secured for orchestral music, theatre, or even film as part of a genuine collective experience. When the Royal Shakespeare Company makes its annual visit to Middlesbrough, it is to perform in a portable theatre erected inside the main sports centre. The event is sold out weeks before the short season. Middlesbrough's Leisure Department has successfully experimented with children's theatre in the main local shopping centres during the annual Middlesbrough Festival, as well as putting on local bands in the new Central Gardens. In nearby Durham the Northern Sinfonia played a concert in the open-air market to an enthusiastic audience of business people, shoppers and town-centre workers, receiving a standing ovation at the end and many letters to the Council of appreciation. The Notting Hill Carnival is now recognized as the largest arts event in Europe. Thamesdown Council has experimented with drive-in movies as part of its annual festival; the open-air relay of opera in Covent Garden from the adjacent Royal Opera House always secures a packed and lively crowd.

The politics of identity

The meaning and identity that people once took from their work they now take increasingly from their leisure interests. The world of the apprenticed or indentured skilled worker who would spend all his or her life in one occupation or firm, of work as a vocation, has almost vanished; work has become less skilled, more casualized, more part-time and contractually short-term. To be defined as a miner, as a train driver, as an engineer, as an embroiderer or as a nurse, is no longer adequate to the identities which people wish to develop in a more mobile and shifting society. Marxist sociologists and market research professionals agree that questions of personal identity are in the melting pot, detached from tradition, class and occupational categories to a large extent. The very demographics of class have changed enormously in the past two decades.

Surveys reported by André Gorz (1989) have revealed that a rapidly growing percentage of employees in Britain, Germany and Scandinavia attach greater importance to their non-working activities than to their paid jobs. This means that leisure activities and choices connected with lifestyles will feature more significantly more in people's lives, and therefore that the choices offered by urban cultures will assume greater strategic importance. The rise and development of feminism from an intellectual movement to a social movement with enormous political and economic implications – more women workers than men, more childcare provision in town centres, more single women parents, more women-only forms of provision – has to be taken on board today by planners, economists, leisure providers and politicians of all political hues. The increased awareness of environmental and health issues is also replete with practical implications for urban policy, from street-cleaning to non-smoking areas, from providing cycle lanes to induction loops in housing offices, from paternity leave to early retirement counselling, from traffic calming to vegetarian menus as a marketing attraction. 'Self-development', according to the Henley Centre for Social Forecasting, is 'expected to become an increasingly important consumer motivation'. An increased demand for fitness and leisure provision, for opportunities to continue some form of education throughout one's whole life, to help others, will all have to be accommodated by the new urban form and the new diversity of town-centre uses and opportunities.

6

The forms of civic renewal

Thus we think of our individual patterns of use in the favourable terms of spending and satisfaction, but of our social patterns of use in the unfavourable terms of deprivation and taxation.

Raymond Williams, Towards 2000 *(1985)*

Private enterprise is good at getting things done, but not at choosing what to do.

Ralph Erskine, architect, The Observer *(1 November 1987)*

An assumption which runs through this book, and the project it is based on, has been that the key actor in the organization and planning of modern urban life has been local government, responsible in its many forms for planning, housing, public transport, highways, social services, education, libraries and amenities, parks and gardens, childcare, play and other services. But, of course, we must acknowledge that what local government can effectively achieve always happens within the context of national government policy and, perhaps most importantly of all, of macroeconomic forces and patterns of wider social change. Many of the towns and cities we looked at were deeply affected by the recession of the late 1970s and early 1980s bringing debilitating levels of unemployment, industrial and land dereliction, a strain on social services, and damaging blows to the morale of local government officers in its wake. The crisis of confidence in local government was everywhere evident.

The changing role of local authorities

The history of local government in England and Wales (a different tradition exists in Scotland) is complex and ever-changing. Corporate local government only came into being in the nineteenth century, the century of political and social reform, with developments such as the creation of local Boards of Health in 1831 to respond to an epidemic of cholera in that year, poor law organization in 1834 resulting in elected Boards of Guardians, the Municipal Corporations Act of 1835 which legitimized some 140 medieval corporations, and later on the Municipal Corporations Act 1882 which redefined the powers and duties of the local boroughs. By the end of the nineteenth century elected urban and rural district councils, metropolitan borough councils and city councils were in place everywhere. As Mark Girouard (1990) noted:

If this book has heroes, they are the corporations of Victorian towns, especially northern industrial towns . . . With unfailing energy and resourcefulness they took over services from inefficient private enterprise, and made them prosperous and fruitful, leaving behind them a rich harvest of town halls, court-houses, market halls, schools, viaducts, bridges, reservoirs, and pumping stations, all proudly flaunting the corporation coat-of-arms from ripely ebullient architecture.

At the beginning of the twentieth century, local government was responsible for almost every aspect of local life: health, education, planning, housing, welfare, and even the provision of gas, electricity and water; many of the service providers were municipally owned public utilities.

Post-war reduction of role

Ironically it was the welfare- and public-service-minded Labour government of 1945 which was the first central government to begin to claw back from locally elected authorities some of their powers: in the name of nationalization and economic efficiency, both health and the municipal utilities were reorganized into national services. It was a Labour government which in 1974 established the Layfield Committee to look into questions of local government finance, a response to the fact that local government expenditure was rising faster than inflation and government was concerned to limit growth in expenditure. Earlier, in 1972, Peter Walker implemented many of the findings of the 1969 Redcliffe-Maud report on local government reorganization to produce five separate kinds of local or regional authority, creating or exacerbating tensions which remain to this day.

In 1980 a Conservative government set up a number of urban development corporations in inner cities with wide powers to bypass normal planning and electoral procedures, along with 22 enterprise zones free of planning restrictions, rates and taxes. In the same year the Housing Act 1980 obliged local authorities to sell off council houses at a discount, and reductions in housing subsidies rapidly slowed down the rate of public housing new starts. The Rates Act 1984 allowed central government, for the first time ever, to determine the level of local authority spending. In 1986 the metropolitan county councils (including the Greater London Council) were abolished; in 1988 the Education Reform Act removed polytechnics from local authority control, allowed schools to opt out, and provided plans for local management of schools including finances. The 1986 Widdicombe Report recommended limiting the rights of local authority employees to stand for election to local councils. The Local Government Act 1988 obliged councils to put many of its services out to tender, and banned certain kinds of 'political' publicity, and the Local Government and Housing Act 1989 sought to control local authority capital expenditure by limiting borrowing, prohibiting the use of capital receipts for reinvestment, and disallowing the subsidizing of housing rents. The poll tax finally reduced all local autonomy in financial control.

The enabling authority

The changes to and extensive limitation of the powers of local government in recent decades have been characterized as a move from the role of direct provision to one of 'strategic and enabling' authorities. The criticism levelled against local authority provision, whether in housing, social services, education, transport or amenities, has been that it has been too standardised, bureaucratic and inefficient. Some of this criticism has had a ring of truth, largely because the electoral process which has brought political parties (of whatever colour) to local power has often been used as an absolute mandate, obviating any further necessity for local consultation or partnership with other bodies. There is still an air of inviolable certainty about many local authority councillors that, having been elected, there is no further need to consult with people or to engage in public debate. Too often decision-makers at local level, whether councillors or officers, have been under-representative of particular local needs and interests. Senior officers rarely travel other than by car; rarely use the town centre for daily shopping; rarely push buggies or wheelchairs through the town centre, and are often commuters to the towns they work in rather than residents.

The proponents of deregulation have argued that, instead of becoming 'bogged down' in the details of actual provision, councillors would spend their time more effectively deciding overall policy and objectives, leaving the actual provision of services to be put out to tender or contracted out to independent or commercial agencies. A recent Secretary of State, Nicholas Ridley, at one point stated publicly that his ideal would be a council which just met once a year to award contracts. The argument seems rational and persuasive, but in practice it is becoming clear that the long-term perspectives of local government – the necessity, for example, to plan for the next generation – often are at odds with the short-term commercial requirements of would-be providers of services. An example of this has been the recent Ninth Report of the Committee of Public Accounts (1991) on the privatization of bus companies, which found that many of the bus stations were immediately sold off for development for commercial uses or shopping rather than retained for public transport purposes. Some accommodation between long-term strategic and infrastructural provision and short-term contracts for certain services is likely to be best.

For in local politics, more than in national politics, party affiliation and ideology are much less evident, and certainly much more responsive to – or derived from – local conditions. In our study, each of the twelve towns – whether Labour, Conservative, Liberal Democrat or with no party in overall control – had a quite individual political 'feel' to it, reflecting regional, class, local historical and demographic factors as much as party affiliation. We quickly learned that not all Labour authorities were highly interventionist or doctrinaire; neither were all Conservative authorities *laissez-faire* or complacent. It is precisely the individual character of each local authority that makes democracy still so pertinent to local government and to continued local differentiation, and produces in almost every authority a range of services and traditions – often including the very good and the very bad within the same town or city – that gives each town or city a unique feel and appearance. It is argued that it is precisely these important differences which would disappear in a welter of privatization and the eventual provision of services by large companies or even international chains. It is bad enough that every high street looks the same; the prospect of every old people's home, social housing complex, swimming pool, park and theatre being developed and managed by the same national commercial company would dispense with local civic identities altogether.

Economic development and tourism

Perhaps the most crucial weakness of local government, certainly in responding to the issues of civic decline which we had identified, was that in most authorities provision was still largely organized along rigid departmental lines – housing, social services, planning, environment, leisure, education and youth services (in the case of unitary authorities) – often with little joint policy work or co-operation between them. And it was often the idiosyncratic way that some services and functions were linked together, with little or no real philosophical or intellectual justification, that made strategic planning difficult if not impossible.

For example, in some authorities library provision came within the remit of education, in others under leisure; nobody could

Towns for people

fully justify either choice. In some leisure departments the sports ethic dominated over the arts ethic and the officers clearly belonged to two different and sometimes antagonistic cultural worlds. Leisure itself has only recently emerged from the empire of the borough engineer, whose job of maintaining the heating levels in the swimming pools was seen as a more germane relationship to leisure than any other. Arts provision, too, in the recent past, has variously been a responsibility of the borough engineer, the director of parks, baths and cemeteries, the borough librarian or the town clerk. The ideology of 'leisure', now one of the main departments in most local authorities, remains largely unexamined. Is it simply about fun or does it have educational or civic implications? Is it mostly to do with organized sports or is it largely about voluntary activity? Is it essentially something that can be bought and sold in the marketplace or is it about fostering communities and associational life? Is it about amateur production or is it about commercial consumption?

In raising these issues we were raising real problems. For it was clear that the question of town-centre decline and the quality of local civic life had disappeared into the gaps between planning, housing, transport and leisure. No one committee or department had been given the task of taking an overall view. There was often no corporate policy, no 'mission statement', no coherent set of policy objectives which informed local authority provision as a whole. Only in recent years has the idea of establishing policy objectives arrived on the agenda of many service departments; one of the strongest criticisms levelled by the Audit Commission (1991) was that in the many towns they looked at, arts and entertainment provision was delivered in a complete policy vacuum, with no agreed set of aims and objectives against which to measure provision.

However, two new developments in local authority provision over the past decade – the necessity of producing economic development, and tourism strategies – have required that corporate strategic thinking becomes essential. Traditionally, economic development was not a part of local government concern or policy, but the recession of the 1970s and 1980s left councillors of all parties greatly concerned about unemployment in their towns. Driven often by a need to be competitive with other towns in attracting new industries or other developments, economic development has become an important new – and potentially cohesive – concern in many councils, and has often moved the authority towards taking a more strategic attitude towards council policy *per se*. Economic drives have led to cultural ambitions, as it has been realized that a key factor in company relocation is often the quality of life in the towns being considered. Preston, Swansea, Middlesbrough and Luton have all given thought to how to attract and retain middle management as part of relocation drives.

The recent development of tourism strategies and policies has often occurred in tandem with economic development. With increased disposable income and time becoming available to many people, councils are competing for this economy with new policies for museums, heritage centres, leisure developments and countryside enhancement programmes. As with economic development, tourism strategies have the potential not only to create jobs, but also to enhance the quality of life for a town's residents as well as its visitors. All tourism strategies start with the question of self-image, and that is as much an indicator of local concern to residents as it is to outsiders. In many towns we found that tourism policies – and initiatives – had been as beneficial to local residents as to visitors. Even local people sometimes need maps, guides and planned entertainment activities.

Yet to date, no local authority we know of has made an explicit policy commitment to improving choice and diversity in social and cultural life in its own town centre in the evenings and at weekends, though many now have this on the agenda. It seems strange to us that such a policy commitment did not naturally precede tourism strategies, and this, of course, was the project we found ourselves engaged in. Some towns are beginning to address these issues in the form of town-centre strategies – Luton, Reading, Middlesbrough and Stirling in particular. Reading has appointed a Town Centre Manager; Middlesbrough refers to such a possibility in its current annual report.

Unfortunately, town-centre strategies are usually driven by land-use matters, so that the policy language and structures to deal with the full scope of diverse town centres do not yet exist.

But the Gulbenkian study (Comedia 1991) itself acted in many places to stimulate discussion about these larger public and civic concerns, and in some places it was within planning departments that a greater readiness to discuss new ideas and create new working partnerships and practices was most evident. Planning policy – so often the immediate target of much criticism of town-centre decline – now seemed the most amenable to debate and democratic consultation.

The planning debate

Patsy Healey (1990) has identified two distinct phases in the ideology of planning in twentieth-century Britain. The first was the *blueprint model*, heavily influenced by developments in technology and civil engineering abetted by social engineering philosophies of progress, which sought to develop urban planning away from nineteenth-century accretion towards large-scale, epic redevelopment. Such a model, Healey argued, 'failed to sustain the self-reflective capabilities which could adjust its role in the light of changing circumstances'. Without building into the planning process the need for consultation, reassessment and monitoring of effects, developments turned into juggernauts that often destroyed the very qualities of human well-being that they were meant to foster.

The second approach Healey called the *rational decision model*; although this built into the planning process forms of consultation, nevertheless it still assumed that planning was essentially always developed at the top and only modified by consultation rather than challenged or abandoned in the face of opposition. The rational model assumed a political consensus, the increased homogenization of lifestyles and patterns of living, the un-problematic increase of social equality, and the willingness of all to fall into conventional ways and geographical zones of work, leisure and home.

Both models have proved inadequate to the complexities of modern life and to the continued diversification of cultures and lifestyles that have arisen as a result of demographic, social and political change. What we now need, Healey insists, is a concept of *planning as debate*, that problematizes all the given facts and policies, assumes political differences, recognizes cultural diversity, and gives equal weight to the wishes of residents, consumers and citizens as it does to the proposals of professional planners and the interests of commercial developers.

A poll conducted by *The Independent* newspaper in April 1990 in response to controversies surrounding the redevelopment of Paternoster Square in London, found, not surprisingly, that 66 per cent of respondents felt that local people should have an important influence in local planning issues; 47 per cent felt the wider public should have an important influence; slightly fewer thought that local council influence should be an important consideration; only 18 per cent thought that central government concerns should wield influence; and finally, only 6 per cent thought that developers should have a major say. This general perception that planning should start from the needs and interests of local people confirms Professor Healey's argument that the time has come to consider seriously future urban planning as a matter for widespread public consultation and debate. In our study of 12 town centres we also frequently came across the perception that much of what had happened in post-war redevelopment had happened without any consultation with local people.

Contract culture: the growth of 'post-democratic' agencies

Yet the problem, as we have seen, in recent decades has been a continued growth away from local decision-making or political influence. The establishment in the 1970s of the Scottish Development Agency and Welsh Development Agency to promote economic growth, while successful, created quangos which were beyond the reach of the Scottish and Welsh political processes. The enterprise zones and the urban development corporations of the 1980s have similarly been imposed by central government as a means of bypassing 'difficult' and often politically hostile local councils. The abolition of the metropolitan county councils in 1986 effectively destroyed the larger urban strategic authorities, and the decrease in central funds to local government, allied with the new Unified Business Rate and the poll tax, have further exacerbated the decline of local political power. Aware of the growing embarrassment (and catastrophic environmental and social effects) of having no London-wide tier of local government, current plans to remedy the situation are more predisposed to an elected mayor and an 'executive' type quango rather than reinstating old-fashioned local elections.

Yet the centralization of decision-making relates not only to the public sector; in the private sector the decline of local economic autonomy has been even more pronounced, as most towns and cities have simply become branch economies of national and international conglomerates. When the Economics Editor of the *Guardian*, Will Hutton, visited Newcastle in the spring of 1991, he reported:

Time and again I was struck how outside decisions over which the North had little influence had suborned local initiative and enterprise. It could be the local Marks & Spencer only having the discretion to contribute £100 to the rehabilitation of the Theatre Royal . . . It could be the clearing banks meeting head-office criteria for limiting lending and widening margins, again with little discretion . . . and closing down swathes of local industry thereby . . . the stripping out of companies with local headquarters by external takeovers and acquisitions, the destruction of the locally owned clusters of engineering and manufacturing companies.

In response there is a jumble of largely un-coordinated agencies, each doing its own thing enthusiastically and well-intentionally – but to no overall vision or purpose.

It is increasingly recognized that the UK is now the exception to a much wider European trend towards the decentralisation of powers, towards the support and development of regional economies and identities, and towards greater political autonomy. Unless there is a reversal of government policy and a revival of local decision-making, the prospect for distinctive and successful urban revitalization based on unique local circumstances is in grave doubt.

What seems to be replacing local government provision and political autonomy is what is now called the 'contract culture'. What was once a unified body of local provision and policy – for good or bad – is becoming a portfolio of dozens of different service contracts, negotiated by different council departments with a variety of commercial firms with little or no reference to each other. Street-cleaning, rubbish collection, housing management, old people's homes, leisure services, public transport, have all been put out to tender in recent years; education has been detached from local government control, and even policing has become increasingly privatized, with more than 1000 policing schemes for housing estates, shopping precincts and other public areas now being run by private companies. In this scenario co-ordination between services – a key ingredient to revitalization – becomes even more difficult.

But the contract culture poses other dangers. For it increasingly encroaches upon not just professional and commercial activities but also local voluntary activity. The Community Development Foundation, in its report, *Taken for Granted* (Chanan 1991), suggests that community activity is an essential part of the continuous unpaid work that people do, and estimates that unpaid work accounts for half or more of all society's work, an importance masked by the conventional definition of 'economic activity'. But as grants begin to turn into contracts, therefore treating the voluntary sector only as a means of service provision, pressures are exerted on those participating in voluntary and community work to abandon their independent activities and philosophies in order simply to become mere agencies of (often unpaid) public provision. This bodes ill for the idea of civil society as a network of independent organizations and interests; instead the vision offered is one of greater centralized demands upon a wide range of companies and organizations servicing local needs but largely fuelled by economic imperatives.

The market may be a more effective means of distributing many goods and services; but what it cannot do, as even the most avid proponents of economic liberalism agree, is provide a vision of community, or suggest how social life and mutual aid can be furthered to avoid the growing anomie that either economic individualism or state dependency produce in civil society.

As Asa Briggs (1968) noted in connection with the growth of the great Victorian cities: 'economic individualism and common civic purpose were difficult to reconcile'. The large council housing estates may have robbed people of the initiative in creating their own mixed communities, but then the emphasis on personal consumption as the main economic motor in the post-industrial society has also done the same: as one person put it, not to have a credit card is these days to be disfranchised from town-centre life.

Civic culture and citizenship

New partnerships

The revitalization of town centres and civic life is likely to be best achieved by co-operation and co-ordination among local government, local businesses and the network of voluntary organizations, interest groups and other community initiatives. The great and abiding strength of local government is that it is elected: if it fails to deliver adequate services or is unresponsive to local needs and interests there is always an opportunity for people to elect it out of office. The strength of the best of the business sector is that it is engaged daily in responding to local, national and international pressures; its business acumen depends on making the most of local conditions to work effectively – to employ people and to mesh into the wider economy of production, distribution and exchange. The voluntary sector provides the social glue that knits individuals together in mutual interest, in caring for each other, and in providing social stability. All three have a common interest in the efficient provision of public services, in a clean and amenable environment in which to work and in a civic and cultural life based on tolerance, diversity and mutual respect.

The importance of cultural policy

We embarked on this study because it was realized that civic culture was in crisis: the growth of domestic leisure, rising street crime, inappropriate town planning, and social and demographic splintering, had produced towns and town centres that people no longer related to other than for daytime shopping. Local councillors and officers, community leaders and business people, beset by economic problems and besieged by political complexity, had failed to develop a new agenda for a diverse, active and participatory civic life. By the end of the study we believed that cultural policy provided the key to a new urbanism, a new way of living in towns that reflected social concerns, enhanced people's self-confidence and identities, and provided the economic wherewithal to prosper and develop. By cultural policy we recognized and understood the prime importance of:

1   the need to respect people's religious, ethnic and historical identities which were often essential to their own sense of self-identity;

2   acknowledging the history, topography and regional identity of the town in which people lived, and the 'cultural' importance of forms of local economic production – the 'Made in Swansea' or 'Made in Gloucester' syndrome;

3   the need to encourage education and self-expression through individual and collective endeavour – involvement in arts and community activities has often preceded wider civic involvement;

4   the need to promote public security and safety through the promotion of mutual respect and tolerance as much as by surveillance and policing;

5   personal well-being and health through involvement in sports and leisure activities, and in group sports and club organizations;

6   the wish to ensure that all people felt able to use the resources locally available to them through outreach programmes, access schemes, special events, schools, further and higher education, libraries, theatres, galleries, concert halls and commercial forms of arts and entertainment;

7   the use of festivals, carnivals, and special events to reclaim public space for local use and for popular activities;

8   overcoming the self-defeating division between amateur arts and crafts (and hobbies) and the professional and commercial forms of provision;

9   encouraging, by twinning programmes, visits, educational exchanges, special interest and community holidays, an interest in other ways of living that in turn encourage local innovation and development;

10 providing that sense of security, awareness and respect for locality, that sense of place, which is essential to psychological well-being and social development.

All of these attributes, then, contribute to what one might call a 'culture of hope' for urban living rather than the culture of despair which seems now to predominate. Attitudes are as important as buildings; individual and social relationships as important as material goods. The city of consumption needs to renew its historic links with the city of production, not just in making goods, but also in creating a public realm of new institutions, activities, festivals and popular debate. Towns and cities in Britain are likely to prosper better by creating greater links and sharing experiences with their counterparts in Europe, than by importing urban regeneration models from the United States, as currently favoured by the present government.

The European experience has deep historical roots in the autonomous city-state tradition of local and regional democracy, of independence from the national centres of power and the national state. On the other hand, the American model offered currently is predicated on the leading role of private finance, of sectoral partnerships and development agencies, and few links with historic local traditions and communities other than through retrospective 'heritage' programmes. Regeneration programmes wholly led by retailing and consumption (the American model is often based on the notion of 'festival retailing') cannot in the long run compensate for urban regeneration based on production, on activity, on fully developed citizenship.

The sense of renewal in Glasgow as a result of preparing the city for its role as European City of Culture in 1990 clearly energized that city and created the sense of a second chance or a fresh start. Many other towns and cities in Britain have been given a new lease of life by the development of new industrial sectors, by conservation projects, tourism initiatives, and the challenge of competing on the European stage in attracting businesses, visitors and infrastructural funding, as clearly evidenced, for example, by Birmingham, Bradford and Sheffield in recent years.

There is no one blueprint for the ideal city, no single action plan, critical path or development brief that can be printed on a transparency and superimposed on the local town plan. Every one of the towns and cities studied was so uniquely different from any other that talk of common solutions became naive. In the end what made them different was that particular relationship between landscape, economic and social history, political traditions and the transformed and transforming character of the people themselves. Cultural renewal starts with the celebration of differences; civic renewal starts by acknowledging the equal right of everybody to participate and have their say.

Bibliography

Anderton, Frances (1989) 'Shopping Mad: The Erosion of Urbanity', *Architectural Review*, May.

Atkins, Stephen (1989) *Critical Paths: Designing for Secure Travel*, Design Council, London.

Audit Commission (1991) *Local Authorities, Entertainment and the Arts*, HMSO, London.

Bell, Daniel (1979) *The Cultural Contradictions of Capitalism*, Heinemann, London.

Bianchini, Franco, Mark Fisher, John Montgomery and Ken Worpole (1988) *City Centres, City Cultures*, Centre for Local Economic Strategies, Manchester.

Bianchini, Franco and Hermann Schwengel (1991) 'Re-imagining the City' in John Corner and Sylvia Harvey (eds) *Enterprise and Heritage*, Routledge, London.

Briggs, Asa (1968) *Victorian Cities*, Penguin, London.

Brookman, Deborah (1990) 'La Plaza del Sol', *a/r/c*, Spring.

Buchan, Keith (1990) *Wheels of Fortune: Transport in the South East*, South East Economic Development Strategy, London.

Buchanan, Peter (1988) 'What City? A Plea for Place in the Public Realm', *Architectural Review*, November.

Burke, Gerald (1976) *Townscapes*, Penguin, London.

Campbell, Bea (1989) 'The Modern Principle', interview with Richard Rogers, *Marxism Today*, February.

Central Statistical Office (1989) *Social Trends 19*, HMSO, London.

Chanan, Gabriel (1991) *Taken for Granted: Community Activity and the Crisis of the Voluntary Sector*, Community Development Foundation, London.

Comedia (1991) *Out of Hours: Summary Report*, Comedia/Gulberkian Foundation, London.

Committee of Public Accounts (1991) *Sales of the National Bus Company, Ninth Report*, HMSO, London.

Crawford, Adam, Trevor Jones, Tom Woodhouse and Jock Young (1990) *The Second Islington Crime Survey*, Centre for Criminology, Middlesex Polytechnic, London.

Dahrendorf, Sir Ralf (1990) 'Does London Need to be Governed?, London Weekend Television London Lecture, December.

Davies, Wendy and Bridget Leach (1991) *Woolwich for Women Survey*, London Borough of Greenwich and Thames Polytechnic, London.

Esher, Lionel (1981) *A Broken Wave*, Allen Lane, London.

Fleming, Roy (1987) 'Lighting and Crime', *Lighting Design*, September.

Francis, Jenni (1991) *The Insider Magazine*, Arts Council, March.

Gardner, Carl and Julie Sheppard (1989) *Consuming Passion: The Rise of Retail Culture*, Unwin Hyman, London.

Girouard, Mark (1990) *The English Town*, Yale University Press, London.

Gorz, André (1989) *Critique of Economic Reason*, Verso, London.

Harvey, David (1989) *The Condition of Post-modernity*, Blackwell, Oxford.

Healey, Patsy (1990) *Planning for the 1990s*, Department of Town and Country Planning, University of Newcastle upon Tyne.

Hillman, Judy (1989) *A New Look for London* (Royal Fine Art Commission), HMSO, London.

Hillman, Judy (1990) 'The importance of the Street', *Town and Country Planning*, February.

Hillman, Mayer and Anne Whalley (1979) *Walking is Transport*, Policy Studies Institute, London.

Jackson, Paul, Tim Maitland and Charles Waterhouse (1990) *The City Centre and the City's Young*, A Report to the Working Party on Disorder in Hull City Centre.

Jackson, W. Eric (1964) *Local Government in England and Wales*, Penguin, London.

Jacobs, Jane (1964) *The Death and Life of Great American Cities*, Pelican, London.

Jukes, Peter (1990) *A Shout in the Street*, Faber & Faber, London.

Landry, Charles *et al.* (1989) *The Last Resort: Tourism Employment and Post-Tourism in the South East*, South East Economic Development Strategy.

Lynch, Kevin (1960) *The Image of the City*, MIT Press, Cambridge, Mass.

Marquand, David (1988) *The Unprincipled Society*, Cape, London.

Matrix (1987) *Making Space: Women and the Man Made Environment*, Pluto, London.

Middleton, Michael (1987) *Man Made the Town*, Bodley Head, London.

Ministry of Transport (1963) *Traffic in Towns: A Study of the Long Term Problems of Traffic in Urban Areas*. Report of the Working Group (Buchanan Report), HMSO, London.

Mintel (1988) *The On Trade Revolution*, Mintel, London.

Montgomery, John (1987) *Trade Winds: The Changing Face of Retail and Retail Employment in the South East*, South East Economic Development Strategy.

Mumford, Lewis (1945) *The Culture of Cities*, Secker & Warburg, London.

Mulgan, Geoff (1989) 'A Tale of New Cities', *Marxism Today*, March.

Mulgan, Geoff and Ken Worpole (1986) *Saturday Night or Sunday Morning?*, Comedia, London.

Murray, Robin (1991) *Local Space: Europe and the New Regionalism*, Centre for Local Economic Strategies, Manchester.

National Consumer Council (1987) Paper at National Chamber of Trade Conference (Janet Graham), 11 October.

Newport Alcohol Abuse and Social Disorder Demonstration Project (1990) Newport, Gwent, February.

Nicholson-Lord, David (1987) *The Greening of Cities*, Routledge & Kegan Paul, London.

Nottingham Safer Cities Project (1990) *Steering Group Report on Community Safety in the City Centre*, Home Office, London.

Planning for Women Group (1987) *Planning for a Safer Environment for Women*, Manchester City Planning Department, November.

Projection 2000 (1990) 'Leisure Centres set to Oust Pubs', *Leisure News*, February.

Raban, Jonathan (1981) *Soft City*, Fontana Collins, London.

Richards, Brian (1990) *Transport in Cities*, Architecture, Design and Technology Press, London.

Rogerson, Robert, Arthur Morris, Allan Findlay and Ronan Paddison (1989) *Quality of Life in Britain's Intermediate Cities*, University of Glasgow.

Sherlock, Harley (1990) *Cities Are Good for Us*, Transport 2000, London.

Smith, David (1989) *North and South*, Penguin, London.

Tuck, Mary (1989) *Drinking and Disorder: A Study of Nonmetropolitan Violence* (Home Office), HMSO, London.

Valentine, Gill (1989) 'The Geography of Women's Fear', *Area*, 21(4).

Ward, Collin (1979) *The Child in the City*, Penguin, London.

Worpole, Ken (1987) *On the Town: A Strategy for Leisure and Choice*, South East Economic Development Strategy.

Working Party on Disorder in Hull City Centre (1990) *Survey of 'Fashion Circuit' Public Houses*, Hull City Council, February.

Index